Donald M. MacKinnon was educated at
Winchester College and at New
College, Oxford. From 1936-37 he was
assistant to the late Professor A. E.
Taylor at Edinburgh University. He
returned to Oxford in 1937 as Fellow
and Tutor in Philosophy at Keble
College, later adding a lectureship at
Balliol College. From 1947-60 he was
Regius Professor of Moral Philosophy at
Aberdeen University, moving in 1960 to
Cambridge as Norris-Hulse Professor of
Divinity and Fellow of Corpus Christi
College, where he remained until he
retired in 1978. He delivered the Gifford
Lectures at Edinburgh University in
1965-66. Professor MacKinnon is a Fellow
of the British Academy and of the Royal
Society of Edinburgh.

THEMES
IN
THEOLOGY

THEMES
—IN—
THEOLOGY
THE THREE-FOLD CORD

Essays in Philosophy, Politics and Theology

DONALD M. MacKINNON
D.D. (Aberdon.), F.B.A., F.R.S.E.

T. & T. CLARK LTD
59 GEORGE STREET
EDINBURGH

Copyright © T. & T. Clark Ltd, 1987.

Typeset by C. R. Barber & Partners, Fort William,
Printed in Great Britain by St Edmundsbury Press Ltd,
Bury St Edmunds, Suffolk and bound by
Hunter and Foulis Ltd, Edinburgh

for

T. & T. CLARK LTD, EDINBURGH.

First printed in the U.K. 1987.

British Library Cataloguing in Publication Data

MacKinnon, D. M.
    Themes in theology: The three-fold cord:
    essays in philosophy, politics and theology.
    1. Philosophical theology
    I. Title
    230'.01   BT40

ISBN 0–567–09446–4

CONTENTS

ACKNOWLEDGEMENTS

The following essays have previously been published in some form. They appear in this collection substantially corrected and revised.

'The Inexpressibility of God', *Theology*, July 1976.

'Kant's Philosophy of Religion', *Philosophy*, April 1975.

'Some Reflections on Time and Space', *Archivio di Filosofia*, 1980.

'Some aspects of the treatment of Christianity by the British Idealists', *Religious Studies*, March 1984,

'Metaphor in Theology', *Scottish Journal of Religious Studies*, Spring 1984.

'Reflections on Mortality', *Scottish Journal of Religious Studies*, Spring 1980.

'Power-politics and Religious Faith', *British Journal of International Studies*, April 1980.

'Creon and Antigone – (Boutwood Lectures 1981)'.
Originally published under the title *Creon and Antigone: ethical problems of nuclear warfare* (Menard Press, 1982).

'The Relation of the Doctrines of the Incarnation and the Trinity', R. W. A. McKinney, ed., *Creation, Christ and Culture* (T. & T. Clark, 1976).

'Prolegomena to Christology', *Journal of Theological Studies*, April 1982.

'Teilhard's *Le Milieu Divin* re-considered'.
Originally published under the title 'Pierre Teilhard de Chardin's *Le Milieu Divin*', *The Modern Churchman*, No. 3 1983.

'Crucifixion – Resurrection'.
Originally published under the title '*Crucifixion – Resurrection. The Pattern of the Theology and Ethics of the New Testament*, by Edwyn Clement Hoskyns, Bart., D.D., and Francis Noel Davey', *Scottish Journal of Religious Studies*, Autumn 1982.

'Edward Schillebeeckx' Christology'.
Originally published under the title '*Jesus: an Experiment in Christology* and *Christ: The Christian Experience in the Modern World* by Edward Schillebeeckx', *Scottish Journal of Religious Studies*, Spring 1981.

INTRODUCTION

At first sight this collection of essays may seem to lack any unity of direction, let alone any discernible common factor present in different degree, in each and every one of them. Yet they are offered as contributions towards a single enterprise, namely the re-construction of the Christian conception of God.

Thus the first group of essays in this collection is occupied with questions belonging to philosophical theology, and in particular the tradition of *theologia negativa*. Agnosticism is certainly further from idolatry than anthropomorphism, and the agnostic less likely than the anthropomorphist to incur condemnation from critical philosopher and from prophet. For the last two (however remote one from another in style) agree in antagonism to those who would make God in their own image. If a middle way is sought in that of analogy, it can only be trodden by those who have put themselves to school on the negative path. Many years ago as strong a champion of the *via analogiae* as the Abbé M. T. L. Pénido insisted that a radical 'épuration des concepts' must precede any confident predication *analogice* in respect of the divine.[1] It can hardly be claimed that the two opening essays in this volume obey Pénido's maxims for such an '*épuration*'; he is no friend of the work of Immanuel Kant, whose influence may be seen in these pages, and not only in the paper treating explicitly of his *Religions-philosophie*. But at least they represent a beginning along the road that may issue men and women in the end into the abyss of the unknown, never precisely to be measured but discernibly not altogether fathomless, an infinite resistant to, yet not ultimately alien to, the reach of understanding. If the language here is metaphorical, this very idiom may justify inclusion of a piece concerned of set

---

[1] See his *La rôle of l'analogie dans la théologie dogmatique* (VRIN)

purpose with the place of metaphor in theology. It should immediately be stated that the scope of that essay would have been broader, and its penetration less obviously superficial, had the writer been more at home in the world of poetry. It might be remarked here that it is no accident that the small publishing house (the Menard Press) which originally published the two lectures entitled *Creon and Antigone* was primarily concerned to issue the work of relatively unknown poets. Greenham Common was never a meeting-place for the philistines in Church and State!

Preoccupation with the limits of human awareness, of the scope of human understanding, is also shown in one way in the reflections on space and time, and in another in the study of the British Idealists, and in another in the deliberately inconclusive essay on human mortality. Where the latter is conceived, it was written under an obsessive pre-occupation with the unwillingness of many writers on the subject of survival to engage with the conditions, both physical and epistemic, under which alone memory is possible for human beings. (An exception is the brief but pregnant discussion of the issue by Dr E. W. Barnes in his unjustly neglected Gifford Lectures on *Scientific Theory and Religion*.[2]) Its conclusion is agnostic, and if faith is invoked in the quotation from Baxter's hymn at the conclusion, it is so invoked because as the later discussion of the material in Hoskyns-Davey' *Crucifixion-Resurrection* suggests, it is an element in authentic Christian faith to emphasize rather than disallow the finality of death.

Where the former essay, treating of space and time is concerned, it may be regarded more as a plea than a contribution. Ignorance of anything more than very elementary mathematics inhibits the author from a proper engagement with the issues of cosmology, and in particular, the

[2] C.U.P., 1933.

transformation of our understanding of space and time. Yet cosmological issues are surely crucial, and what Teilhard de Chardin offered in outline in *Le Milieu Divin* (discussed elsewhere in the volume), requires to be worked out in more comprehension and demanding detail. We await the arrival of the *Pascal de nos jours*.

'All power tends to corrupt; absolute power corrupts absolutely'. These often misquoted words of Lord Acton may serve to introduce the seemingly very different essays treating of the problems raised by the use of power in the world of international politics. The one is primarily historical and reflective, the latter contemporary and openly controversial. In both a theological note may be heard, different, perhaps markedly different, in the two cases. But their presence in this collection should advertise the extent to which any serious theological work must take account of the over-all ecclesial, and human context in which it is carried on. There is, after all, a direct line discernible from the acclaim with which Constantine's so-called 'conversion' was received, and the continued unwillingness of very many in the Christian Churches to ask themselves whether their whole understanding of the relations of Christ and Caesar does not need re-thinking. It is not of course that such relations today are in any way homogeneous. Thus it is merely frivolous to suggest that the situation in which 'Liberation' theologians[3] in Latin America are working is akin to that faced by Anglican theologians in a Church of England still 'by law established'. Yet both alike are, or in the latter case, should be, conscious of an inheritance that cripples at least as much as it enables the workings of the Holy Spirit of God. In Scotland the memory of the Disruption of 1843 still seems, at least to an Anglican observer, a source of

[3] These words are in no way intended in criticism of the fundamentally significant work these theologians are doing.

genuine inspiration, of an awareness that the hour may come when in Christ's name, the word 'no' must be spoken for all to hear. 'There is something intolerably paradoxical in the notion of a war to make the world safe for Christianity'. These words were written in 1937 by a Roman Catholic woman, who was shocked by the manner in which her co-religionists espoused the cause of General Franco during the Spanish Civil War. It is very easy to suppose that because Christianity, as we know it, has been received as part of the familiar structure of our daily lives, Christian faith demands for its perpetuation, the external guarantee of its constitutional embodiment. And it is, of course, in the range of problems, raised by the methods of modern warfare, that these issues achieve an obviously focal definition.

A proper treatment would certainly probe much more deeply than either of these essays attempts to do, the significance and rôle of power in human life. It may well be thought that this is an area in which the Churches have all in one way or another failed, either by accepting uncritically the attitudes and standards of the society around them, or of certain strata within it, or else by a kind of half-deliberate aversion from the problems raised, and decisions become necessary, by means of their own involvement with the power-structures around them. In this century few, if any, theologians have engaged more deeply with these issues than Reinhold Niebuhr, and it is greatly to be hoped that more attention will be paid in the future to his wide-ranging and always searching reflections on their ramifications. But in my own personal judgement, we have to reckon with a continuing impoverishment of fundamental theological thought, springing from excess reverence for the powers that be as ordained of God. Yet forty years after the completion of its labours, the verdicts of the International Military Tribunal at Nuremberg on some of the defendants, serve as a very salutary reminder that obedience to superior orders may sometimes be offered in excuse for infamy, only to have its validity even as an excuse, rejected with the clear implication that there are situations in which revolt rather than acceptance is authentic virtue.

If there is confusion here, it is no accident that the lectures entitled *Creon and Antigone* end with some reflections on Christ's ordeal in the desert. It is to such crucial moments in the received tradition of Christ's life that we must, in my judgement, return for fundamental illumination, and we must do so in a style subtly different from that characteristic both of the 'old' and the 'new quest' for the historical Jesus. Here indeed is the link between this group of essays and those that follow. Here also perhaps a certain over-all unity of purpose may be discerned. The essays are not apologetic except in the restricted sense of urging the need for the reconstruction rather than the abandonment of the traditional scheme of Trinity and Incarnation. The problems of such an enterprise are immense, so large that one is often tempted to reject the undertaking as sterile or worse. Yet the figure of Christ in its concreteness, its tragedy, its mystery still beckons, and one's gratitude to the Churches springs from the fact that in spite of their continuing historical infidelity to His inspiration, His Spirit's presence has enabled them to bear witness to the secret of His ways. We need to-day a kind of radicalism of vision that will renew our perception, even as our understanding is deepened.

This final group of essays may be judged to be informed by a dual impatience: an impatience with those who shrink from the intellectually demanding task of reconstruction, preferring the quickly delivered fruits of a facile reductionism, and an impatience with those who cover with a blandly knowing smile, their unwillingness to re-think *ab initio* the proper relations of ecclesia and state. On occasions one notices that a readiness to jettison much that might be thought central to traditional Christian belief goes hand in hand with a tired institutional conservatism. Indeed the former is sometimes invoked to buttress the latter, as if the irreformability of the structures alone provided security against the volatility of faith. But it is by their faithful witness to the *Mysterium Christi*, through word and teaching, through worship and sacrament, that those very structures must be judged, and if found wanting, swiftly rejected. There are very many ways in which that witness may be trivialized, and one of them assuredly that of making churchly existence an end in itself.

Although a powerful and indeed impressive element in contemporary English theological thought tends towards a non-Trinitarian conception of God, and the corresponding diminution of the force of traditional conciliar Christology, it is different on the continent of Europe, where the names of Eberhard Jüngel, Jürgen Moltmann and Hans Urs von Balthasar in very different ways one from another, attest the vitality of other styles of thought. Moltmann and Balthasar differ in much; the former may be judged deficient in metaphysical analysis, the latter undisciplined in the exercise of a profound theological imagination. (Such charges are in my view disputable.) But they are engaged on work of fundamental reconstruction, free from obsessive domination by the supposed need to choose in Christology between arguing from below upward, or from above downward. How desperately we need a Trinitarian exegesis of the 'Sermon on the Mount', and how unlikely to receive it, apart from the radicalization of theological perception to which in very different ways, the theologians I have mentioned are contributing!

The work that these essays represent is quite incomplete. The omissions, especially perhaps the total failure to do justice to the inheritance of other world-religions, of Islam, of Buddhism, of Hinduism is manifest. (At least the memory of the Holocaust must for ever forbid the Christian to forget the awful mystery of Israel.) But their unity, such as it is, may be focused in a sustained plea for Christological renewal, metaphysically, exegetically, practically disciplined, for a perception of the *Mysterium Christi*, that only a quite new fusion of intellectual and scholarly honesty with practical, personal commitment, of metaphysical thought both rigorous and questioning with sense of human frailty and limitation can make possible. And the inclusion of two lectures entitled *Creon and Antigone* should serve at this point to remind the reader that *sub specie temporis*, a definitive solution must remain something unimaginatively remote.

Old Aberdeen
January/February 1986   D. M. MacKinnon

PART A

Chapter I

THE INEXPRESSIBILITY OF GOD

The bitter argument between Moses and Aaron which is at the heart of Schoenberg's opera reaches its climax before the golden calf. In the second scene of the second act Aaron yields to the people's demand that he restore their old gods to them in a comprehensible, a visually perceptible, form. He has himself tried to win time by the ambivalent suggestion that Moses' god may have forsaken or destroyed him. I call the suggestion ambivalent; for if Aaron is only half serious in what he says, in so far as he *is* half serious, he draws on his sense that Moses' god is altogether strange, alien, inscrutable. He *might* destroy, or hide himself so totally that even a servant as devoted to his god's cause as Moses might feel himself forsaken. But Aaron's suggestion makes the people's demand totally irresistible and from their treasures the golden calf is fashioned. The golden calf will neither forsake nor destroy, as Moses' god *might*; this is because it is wonderfully made to measure. Of course in the third scene of the second act, as the momentum increases, so the suggestion is plain that moral disintegration follows the abandonment of the god of the commandments. The calf is fashioned of precious materials, given freely, indeed most generously, by those who would have their god set forth before them in an object at once precious and made to measure. Aaron seemingly knew what he was about, seeking to meet the religious needs of an ill-assorted horde of human beings. It is not only that he knew that those, whom he led, loved to have it so; he did not see how because they were human beings of flesh and blood, committed in hope of their future destiny to a desperate journey, they could be expected to be faithful to the god who had called on them thus to travel, unless (in some way or other) they had him before their eyes.

Of such accommodating pastoral concern Moses will have no part. Although he can say nothing of the god whose commandments he conveys, he *knows* that the god of the Aarons of this world is no god at all. He knows that the god they embody in their idol will indulge them in ways that will ultimately undermine and pervert their sensibility; he recognizes the dangers in the people's cry for a god that they can see with their eyes, hear with their ears, touch with their hands, indeed distinguish at a glance from all that they would quickly write-off as other than he.

We are here in contact with a great and persistent theme of metaphysical theology. The Hebrew prophets of the eighth century B.C. and their successors took up, in their small, disturbed and often terribly threatened worlds, the great emphases of Moses's argument. In later centuries, in the very different settings of the schools, it became a commonplace that in speech about God, we continually swing between an anthropomorphism that ultimately reduces the divine to the status of a magnified human worldly reality, and an agnosticism which continually insists that where God is concerned, we may only confidently affirm that we do not know what we mean when we speak of him; nor indeed do we know how the concepts we apply to him latch onto his being, borrowed or developed as they are from the familiar world of our experience. Always agnosticism was judged less perilous than anthropomorphism.

We often hear quoted the remark of Thomas Aquinas to the effect that of God we know that he *is*, what he is *not*, and what relations everything other than himself has to him. We are clear what he is not. To illustrate, let me refer first to the divine knowledge which the psalm-writer celebrated, mentioning especially the way in which the secrets of the human heart, the hidden depths of human motive and unacknowledged purpose, lay open to God.

> Such knowledge is beyond my understanding;
> so high that I cannot reach it.

and continuing:

> Thou knowest me through and through:
> my body is no mystery to thee,
> how I was secretly kneaded into shape
> and patterned in the depths of the earth.

Of course we have all of us met human beings who have become exceptionally skilful in penetrating the secrets of the human heart, and who also have come in a measure to understand themselves. Yet such human beings have won knowledge of themselves and of others only by long and exhausting experience, critically reflected on. Also their most confident judgements are usually safeguarded by a marginal qualification, leaving room for modification in the light of further experience. But the divine knowledge of which the psalmist writes is altogether otherwise. Here painful scrutiny, whether of oneself or of the others whose secrets one must try to reach, has no place at all. The psalmist speaks of the transparency of the creature to its creator, a transparency that obviates the need to use any sort of conceptual apparatus to spell out to the learner what he would wish to make his own.

Similar principles apply when we seek to conceive God's knowledge of the universe. Take the methods involved in empirical cosmology, where the horizons of our understanding of the origins of the universe are surely being pushed back (though not without sharp argument and controversy); or think of general propositions concerning the microphysical structure of the external world to which we belong and of which indeed we are part, which dazzle those who can grasp their significance by their comprehensiveness, their conceptual economy, their simplicity, their very elegance. Yet such propositions remain completely vulnerable to refutation by what, in the last resort, our senses reveal to us. We know that our greatest intellectual triumphs are, in a perfectly intelligible way, always at risk. There are certain built-in factors, constantly operative, with which we must always reckon—openness to correction, difficulty in the way of proper assimilation of the import of some new theoretical advance etc. Part indeed of what we understand by characteristically human knowledge is defined by reference to these limitations, this framework within which, for instance, the spontaneous creativity, the brilliant mathematical inventiveness of the theoretical physicist is exercised. It was Einstein himself who insisted that while spontaneous intellectual creation was sheerly indispensable to advance in the field of theoretical understanding, it was a grave mistake to suppose that by such creation we reached the secret essence of physical reality, as if thought had unlimited penetrative power to reach behind the world we perceive and with which we have to do every day; with which indeed the innovations in question will help us to deal in unprecedentedly novel styles.

God's knowledge has nothing in common with the human knowledge of which I have spoken. The limitations that express its fundamental disciplines have no place where his omniscience is concerned. What then is the point of speaking of his knowledge, his omniscience? Do we do more than advertise his total freedom from limitation that we have to acknowledge as soon as we begin to reflect seriously on what is involved for human beings in coming to know? Can we indeed significantly speak of God as knowing? It was a commonplace of the medieval schools to insist that God did not belong in any *genus* or sort, that it was a radical mistake to speak of him as *a* substance, even as *a* totally unique substance. We could, (using Boethius' language) speak of him as the 'very ocean of substance', and so acclaim him the originating fount of the substantial. By substantial here we mean that which exists of itself, and to which all other forms of being, property, accident, relation, deprivation and the rest are relative and subordinate. But what of this origination compared with that with which we are familiar in the natural world and in the world of human affairs? We may seek to characterize it as the difference between that which is absolute and that which is relative; but what can we say of that difference? How does it resemble the difference between jersey cows and friesians, between men and women, between sounds and colours, or between the world of the pure mathematician and the world of the historian or if you like between universals and particulars, between essence and existence? Is it any kind of difference? Do we have the right to speak of difference here as if absolute and relative could be compared and therefore validly brought on to the sort of level on which we need to set things in order to distinguish them?

Let us turn now to God's eternity. In prayer, men and women speak of the God of Abraham, Isaac and Jacob, that is of Moses' God, as 'the one before whom the generations rise and fall'. The idiom implies that successive generations of men and women are simultaneously present to the absolutely immutable. For him the distinction between past, present and future has no significance of any sort whatsoever. Rather he is as he is to our forefathers; he is as he is to those who are yet unborn. In certain moods men and women find this eternity a source of consolation; but in doing so they are perhaps in imagination identifying it with resistance to change, enduring immunity from its impact. They are reducing the divine eternity to terms of the recognizable. Let me explain.

We are all of us familiar with the hackneyed image of the hills that remain more or less as they are across the centuries. Yet when men call God the 'ancient of days', it is not to acclaim him as the oldest of all. For by such an acclamation he would be confined within the frame of time, imagined almost as a living mountain. We can of course go some way towards spelling out the sense of God's transcendence by this image. We represent him as uninvolved in the changes and chances of human life and therefore maybe as possessing the resources required to intervene even at the deepest level. Of course the notion of a mountain alive, responding to need, is a fantastic one.

If we do conceive this ever-enduring mountain, powerful by reason of its immunity from involvement in the world to succour as well as to protect, this image does not free us from temporal definition. Indeed we might say that omnipresence as well as eternity is lost. For if a living mountain is represented as having a history, even a very long one, it must also have a place.

So to free ourselves from the tyranny of images that necessarily diminish the divine to the level of the supra-human, we move towards aphasia. We speak of a knowledge that is conceivable simply in terms of the absence of all those conditions that in our world help to distinguish human knowledge from credulity, valid belief from superstition. What is this knowledge that requires no discipline for its achievement? And what is this eternity that if it is actual seems to strip the eternal of any possibility of significant relation to the temporal? It is true that Augustine spoke of time as coming to be with creation, implying that succession is the fundamental order of the world. But what can we say of the creator's awareness of the succession? We all of us know cases of what we call synoptic vision in which the items seen together as a pattern succeed one another in time. We can go on conceiving more and more inclusive examples of such synopsis. Yet still these synopses are selective; they enable us to view as wholes particular stretches of time that are unified by reason of the pattern we find in them. But these stretches which we regard as wholes are still themselves parts of a greater totality.

In Schoenberg's opera, Moses and Aaron are in sharp conflict. Yet in the third act for which the composer wrote the text, Moses tells the soldiers to set Aaron free. 'If he can, let him live' he says. But Aaron drops dead. And we are left wonderng whether this was what Moses wanted. Or is he all the time almost in spite of himself afraid of Aaron? The kind of God that we approach by the pitiless negation of all that we find ourselves moved to say about him easily emerges as a God whose infinity renders him indifferent to the very distinction between good and evil on which Moses lays such weight. Must we not suppose such a God somehow absent from the play of the children of Israel about the calf they have made? Or if not absent, somehow deliberately in his creative will, suspending them from being, in such a way that their sport becomes somehow unreal in his sight? We can be sure that Moses would condemn such metaphysical conceit as furiously as the worship of the calf itself. For Moses' god is one who exacts and enforces obedience to his commandments.

None can question Moses' claim to represent a religion of an austerity incomparably grander than the comforting, indulgent worship Aaron believed that human nature craved. It is an austerity of unquestionable intellectual as well as moral grandeur. Yet has not Moses his own problem to face? He will not allow that his God can be represented or defined; yet his God is able to impose his will, even to communicate that will to his true servants that they may let others know what he commands. Of course the first and greatest commandment is that God should be acknowledged for what he is and the crucial step in this acknowledgement is the refusal to fashion any image of his being. It is almost as if God's first commandment were that where he is concerned, men and women should be silent.

Yet when Moses speaks of God as commanding, is he not himself guilty of anthropomorphism? In the Book of Common

Prayer, in prayer for the sovereign, God is addressed as 'high and mighty, king of kings, lord of lords'. The imagery is obvious; God's omnipotence is represented after the likeness of the supremacy 'over all causes, ecclesiastical as well as temporal' which Henry VIII asserted throughout his dominions when he made himself 'head of the Church'. God's sovereign power is represented after the likeness of that of an identifiable historical despot. There is the same levelling down of the transcendent to the form of a magnified, supra-human reality. Of course the image is terrifying rather than consoling; it is of one who is lawgiver, witness, judge, executioner, endowed with a majesty before which men tremble and in whose recollection they find no excuse of self-indulgence, remembering the account that they must make, are indeed constantly making. But is this conception any less an image than Aaron's conforming, consoling, too humanly human idol? If Aaron the priest trivializes the worship of God to the level of devotion to a godling who will condone every human weakness and indulgence, does not Moses the prophet make of him a judge whose remorseless authority will give the prophet the ground on which he needs to stand in order to lash the frailties of a humanity which the prophet shares with those whom he would guide? Must he not also accept for himself the discipline of silence, even admit with a smile that the Aarons of this world help administer such discipline?

And yet in the end Moses comes himself to acknowledge how desperately difficult such discipline must be, almost from the beginning doomed to total failure. If silence concerning the ways and being of God is received as his command, by being so received, it is received as the fiat of an ultimate. Therefore that which supposedly comes from that ultimate is received after human measure. So Moses states but does not solve the central religious problem of a silence that is properly adequate to the one of whom nothing can be properly said.

Did others who came after him say any more concerning the proper inexpressibility of God? It is interesting to notice the extent to which the mystics adopted the image of the darkness into which Moses entered and distinguished that darkness (their own) from that of, for instance, a guilt-induced despair. And there is also for the Christian the strange and perhaps hardly explored silence of Christ in his passion. Perhaps it is a central task of theology in this day and generation to face anew the question what sort of silence, what sort of repudiation of every sort of image best conveys the ultimacy not of judgement but of love. Yet when I say this, I immediately remember that the authentic simplicity of love is quickly lost and that, in consequence, if we refer to divine love we are using a term whose human currency is very often debased and in very different ways. It is therefore only within the context of the most rigorous discipline of silence that we dare think such a reality.

This essay is a slightly amended version of a talk broadcast in the intervals of concert performances of Schoenberg's opera Moses and Aaron—*in 1974 and 1975.*

Chapter 2

KANT'S PHILOSOPHY OF RELIGION

It was in 1792 that Kant published the first Book of his most important single work on the philosophy of religion—*Religion within the Limits of Reason Alone*. But it was his very interesting treatment of the biblical material in the second Book that involved the philosopher in his one serious conflict with official authority. Greene and Hudson give a good account of this conflict and its effect on the work as a whole in the introduction to their translation of *Religion* in the Harper Torchbook Series (1960).[1]

The work appeared eleven years after the first edition of the *Critique of Pure Reason*, and it belongs with the last of Kant's major writings. Thus it takes for granted certain fundamental tracts of the philosopher's sustained argument, for instance the deeply critical evaluation of the transcendent metaphysical impulse, formulated in the Dialectic of the first *Critique*, and significantly developed in the extended treatment of such topics as the complementarity of mechanical and teleological explanation in the *Critique of Judgment*, the so-called 'primacy of practical reason' and the related doctrines of the unconditional authority of the moral law and the autonomy of the rational human subject. The student of Kant's theory of knowledge, and criticism of metaphysics, and the student of his ethical and political theory, both alike find in his work on religion a great deal that is continuous with arguments with which they are familiar, and that throws new light on the substance of Kant's

[1] All page references in this article are to this translation: likewise all quotations are from it.

principles by revealing their implications when they are applied to the task of the critical evaluation of religious practices and *credenda*. But there is more to be said.

Three years after the publication of the first edition of the *Critique of Pure Reason*, Kant published an opusculum in which he attempted to answer the question: *Was ist Aufklärung?* It was indeed within the tradition of the *Aufklärung* that he stood, and he wrote as one convinced that the moral obliquity involved in the torture, imprisonment, and deprivation of civil rights of a religious antagonist, who found himself or herself conscientiously unable to subscribe to one or other of a number of competing systems of *credenda*, possessed or should possess a quite unmistakably greater evidence than any of the *credenda* in question. By invocation of such methods, those who had recourse to them mutilated their own moral dignity as well as that of their victims. If Hume depreciated the 'monkish virtues', Kant was sharply alert to the sort of unacknowledged self-regard that lurked beneath the intellectual rigour and ascetic austerity of the inquisitor. So we find him before 1792, committed, as it were, in advance to a particular sort of reductionist approach to the problems of the philosophy of religion. It is not one in which religious and theological conceptions are eliminatively defined in ethical terms: rather Kant sought to bring the world of religion under that of ethics. In *Religion* itself we find such impulses strongly at work in the treatment of grace and prayer. But it is not the whole story. Even if we do no more than attend to the controversial introductory section of *Religion*, which treats of 'radical evil', we cannot fail to recognize that it is in this section of a work which is concerned with the critical analysis of specifically religious *credenda*, that Kant makes quite explicit the deep moral pessimism, of which students of the *Grundlegung* are continually vaguely aware, and which is also reflected in the openly avowed Hobbism of the essay *On Perpetual Peace*. It is deeply significant that it is in his major work on religion that Kant shows himself so uncompromisingly antagonistic to the facile, perfectibilist aspirations discernible in some (though not in all) writers usually claimed to belong to the Enlightenment. And as we shall see in other respects too Kant's philosophy of religion is very far from reductionist.

In this essay I want to discuss three questions: (a) the treatment of the relation of religion and ethics in Kant's philosophy; (b) the significance of certain individual passages both for Kant's philosophy as a whole and for the philosophy of religion and the philosophy of theology, and (c) the bearing of Kant's philosophy of religion on his criticism of transcendent metaphysics and the distinction, so mercilessly criticized by Professor Strawson, between phenomena and 'things in themselves'.

(a) In his work *On Religion*, Kant is concerned primarily with religion as a separable aspect of human life. He treats it as, in fact, the name of a family of practices including here a number of beliefs, but beliefs regarded essentially as subordinate to the practices which they both inculcate and/or sustain. For him religion has an extractible form; although, writing when and where he did, he inevitably treated most extensively of Christianity, he is drastically criticized by Hegel for his failure to attend closely enough to the particularities of individual religious traditions, including here the historical circumstances in which they were born, developed and took the determinate shapes that they did. Kant is almost entirely innocent in this section of his work of any historical sense. I say almost entirely, remembering that in his essay *On Perpetual Peace* ideas are in play which are also important in his specific treatment of religion.

It is often said that his attitude towards prayer shows that Kant was deeply insensitive to characteristically religious impulses. In his ethical writing he so stresses human autonomy that he finds in the attitude of the devout, who seem to seek from the hand of God what they should achieve for themselves, something destructive of the very substance of moral life. If men are moral agents, what they do must be their own; his style is Stoic and he offends even those who altogether reject the claims of religion, by his seeming indifference alike to humility, to tenderness and to weakness. I say seeming indifference because here, as always, one quickly becomes aware that Kant tries to do justice to what at a first reading he seems to dismiss out of hand. He writes admittedly as a philosopher with a clear vision of the moral life and his own personal sense of the priorities within it. Further, although he is indifferent to historical relativity, he is himself (as I have said) a man of the age in which he wrote and his work on religion is only intelligible if these facts are remembered.

Where the moral life is concerned, it is notorious that Kant is unwilling under any circumstances to consider a lie justified, even if the extremity of the situation in which the lie is told might be thought casuistically to make of words spoken a kind of performance designed, for instance, to protect a friend from the secret police rather than a misrepresentation of fact. One could speak in such a case of a verbal feat carried out in full awareness that one was conveying false information concerning one's friend's whereabouts, a feat executed in full awareness of what one is doing. It seems moral pedantry on Kant's part to fail to distinguish (as Plato does) such an action from one in which one's deceit involves, however slightly, the kind of self-deception which Kant would seem to have feared as inevitably destructive of the sort of relationship he supposed human beings must try to establish with themselves and with their fellows. If a man deliberately hides what he is actively about not only from his fellows but in a measure from himself (and it is Kant's view that the liar must do this), he puts the 'realm of ends' in peril, and of this 'realm' he is himself as much a member as the man or woman to whom he tells an untruth.[2] We must, as far as is possible, learn what we are about when we act. If Kant notoriously insists that the moral worth of an action depends upon the motive from which it is done and sometimes seems to identify this motive with respect for a moral law itself identified with the achievement of a mere formal consistency of maxim, in other places (even in the *Grundlegung*) he clothes this consistency with flesh and blood, at least delineating the kind of order he supposes we achieve by a relentless refusal to allow any purposes, whether individual or collective, to distract us from submission to the sovereign authority of the 'realm of ends'. Sometimes Kant is betrayed by his argument into writing as if the whole of morality consisted in our being honest with ourselves and as if immorality was found in any action that deterred us, or threatened to deflect us, from submission to the rigorous dictates of such a policy of life. Yet, if he moves in such a direction he does so because he is aware that men are often deceived into supposing that they cease to be self-regarding by subordinating their private individual purposes to a collective. Thus the soldier, obeying the dictates of an allegedly superior authority to serve in the forces of his country in an unjust war, or persuaded by patriotic sentiment to remain silent when the methods by which a war just in the circumstances of its inception is prosecuted, become destructive of the ends it has been initiated to achieve, cannot obviously be accused of self-regard. But the cause he is serving is one expressive of an uncriticized collective self-seeking that would seem to silence individual protest against its procedures in the name of the moral order by regarding its actions as themselves creative of the only system of imperatives an agent needs, in the special circumstances indicated, to guide his conduct aright.

When Kant wrote on the relation of religion and ethics, he

---

[2] Cf. Butler's sermon on *Self-Deception*.

wrote (as I said above) as a man who was vividly aware of the extent to which religious authorities, claiming to declare the ways of God to men, were wont to identify obedience to their reading of the alleged divine purpose or purposes with ultimate human good. In particular they had shown themselves as a matter of historical fact totally unwilling to exercise any sort of restraint upon the methods which they employed to enforce conformity with their doctrine and tradition. Granted that they acted in the conviction that the matters on which they claimed to speak were of crucial import, they allowed this conviction to betray them (as I said above) into the worst conceivable violations of human integrity. In doing this, they showed themselves oblivious of the collective self-interest which, unknown to them, shaped their actions. When Acton remarked that 'all power tends to corrupt, absolute power corrupts absolutely', he wrote as one who had clearly learnt a moral lesson that Kant certainly believed to be of the greatest importance. To understand Kant's ethics, and especially his view of the relations of ethics to religion, it is most important to realize that he develops his often curiously elusive ethical ideas in part at least as a protest against the morally destructive effects wrought on human life by competing religious authoritarianisms. It is not that he regarded the questions on which devoutly religious men and women differed one from another as trivial or even as impossible of settlement. It is rather (to repeat myself again) that he supposed the moral outrage committed by any attempt to impose one set of beliefs against another as more evident than any of the competing systems. He has indeed a good deal to say that is sometimes very interesting on various technical theological issues; but he says it in the context of a clear conviction that moral principles are sovereign and that if any form of religion is to be acknowledged valid, it can only be one that does not dispute this sovereignty.

Yet Kant does not go on from there simply to evaluate

religious *credenda* as so many aids to living well. It is a pity that some of those who write on his so-called 'moral argument for the existence of God' do not pay more attention to his writing on religion. It is clear from the argument of the Dialectic in the first *Critique* that he did not regard the kinds of proposition we might suppose the yield of such an argument as intelligible. Similarly, where immortality is concerned, the conclusions he claims to have reached in the Paralogisms of Rational Psychology remain; we can attach no sense to what we may say concerning a surviving substantial soul. Where Kant speaks of the immortality of the soul as a 'postulate of pure practical reason', by doing so he makes of immortality matter primarily of rational religious *hope*. It is, moreover, a hope that he supposes justified by the fact that only if we entertain the idea of a state in which frustrations to the completion of the individual's moral commitment are made good, are we confirmed in the commitment in question. We must not forget here the impact upon the intellectual world to which Kant belonged of the Lisbon earthquake of 1755. It was not only the crude metaphysics of those who argued this to be the 'best of all possible worlds' that received a heavy blow from this disaster. The circumstances in which men and women met their deaths reminded such a philosopher as Kant that if indeed 'ought implies can', he must reckon with the seeming total indifference of the environment in which men and women lived towards the sort of moral self-discipline, the sort of strenuous struggling after honesty, on which he laid such emphasis. Questions were raised concering the relation of the 'realm of nature' to the 'realm of ends' to which theoretical answers were already ruled out as inconceivable. But men and women were creatures of flesh and blood, and if they were to pursue the good life, especially as Kant conceived it, they must have some sort of assurance that their labour was not in vain. Of course, in order not to misconceive such assurance, they must first find themselves convinced of the sovereign authority of the moral order. In other words, they must receive the categorical imperative as categorical. It may be that Kant here advances into sheer self-contradiction. If he can be thought to escape such a charge, we must try to integrate what he is emphasizing in the passages in his writings at present in my mind with the central problem left by the *Critique of Pure Reason* of the relation of phenomena to 'things in themselves' with which I shall be concerned in the last part of this essay. For the time being, I would emphasize that for all his explicitly affirmed hostility to the life of prayer, it is as an eschatological hope entertained in the practice of religion subordinated to morality that we dare to speak of immortality. *But what can we say of such entertainment?*

Where the hope of immortality is concerned, Kant is primarily (in my view) moved by consideration of the natural evils (*Übel*) that menace moral practice, including (one might add) circumstances of inheritance and early environment for which children cannot conceivably be held responsible: (it is indeed at this point that we touch the frontiers between *Übel* and *Böse* (moral evil)). If Kant was blind where prayer was concernded, he did his utmost to make sense of grace. A recent French writer on Kant's philosophy of religion (M. Bruch)[3] has indeed suggested that the tag of the Jesuit theologians, *Facienti quod in se est, non denegat Deus gratiam*, goes a long way to express concisely Kant's understanding of the way in which alleged divine grace co-operates with human freedom. There must be found in the agent a kind of prior responsiveness to the divine perfecting and transforming of his or her action. Again, there is a frankly Stoic emphasis on individual effort; it is indeed this note of strenuous moral endeavour that is found deeply uncongenial by many students of Kant's ethics. This, though the unexpected emphasis on what he calls 'radical evil' in *Religion*

---

[3] In his book *La Philosophie Réligieuse de Kant* (Aubier, 1970).

goes some way to lay bare the pessimism out of which some of the characteristic emphases of his moral philosophy sprang. While emphasizing in his philosophy of religion the subordination of religion to morality to the extent of insisting that characteristically religious conceptions find their sense in a moral context, he is yet equally emphatic that where some of these conceptions (for instance, even that of divine grace) are concerned, they have a content that cannot be exhaustively cashed in moral terms. But what is this content? Can we attach any sense to it? Here Kant seems to require at the same time to invoke the sort of metaphysical agnosticism he claimed to establish by his distinction of phenomena from things in themselves and an almost indulgent readiness to use conventional religious language, as if the combination of his agnosticism with his moralism would protect men and women against misunderstanding what they were about in using it.

To make my meaning clearer I venture to quote a prayer:

> O God, the God of the spirits of all flesh, who by a voice from heaven didst proclaim, Blessed are the dead which die in the Lord, multiply, we beseech thee, to those who rest in Jesus, the unsearchable blessings of thy love, that the good work which thou didst begin in them may be perfected unto the day of Jesus Christ (Scottish Book of Common Prayer, 1929).

I am not for one moment suggesting that Kant would have approved the religious sentiments expressed in that prayer. A very great deal that he says on the subject of human autonomy is incompatible with the implied confession of the divine origination of the good that allegedly has been done by those on whose behalf the prayer is offered. Yet consider the following passage:

> That is, he can hope in the light of that purity of the principle which he has adopted as the supreme maxim of his will, and of

its stability, to find himself upon the good (though strait) path of continual *progress* from bad to better. For Him who penetrates to the intelligible ground of the heart (the ground of all maxims of the will) and for whom this unending progress is a unity, i.e. for God, this amounts to his being actually a good man (pleasing to Him); and, thus viewed, this change can be regarded as a revolution. But in the judgment of men, who can appraise themselves and the strength of their maxims only by the ascendancy which they win over their sensuous nature in time, this change must be regarded as nothing but an ever-enduring struggle towards the better, hence as a gradual reformation of the propensity to evil, the perverted cast of mind.[4]

In the lay-out of *Religion* the passage occurs after the sombre introductory exposition of 'the radical evil in human nature'. The account which Kant gives of the origin of this tendency (if he allows that any account can be given at all, in terms intelligible to us) is very obscure (p. 38). In the passage quoted, however, he is clearly insisting that where human appreciation of the moral life is concerned, any overcoming of this evil tendency, whether in oneself or another, must be represented as a temporal progress. Yet mindful presumably of his arguments in the *Critique of Pure Reason* aimed at showing both that time is genetically a subjective form of intuition, and at the same time the all-embracing context both of our experience and of the world with which in that experience we have to do, he suggests that we cannot conceive how such a progress may be viewed from the divine standpoint. Yet where we are concerned, it is of moral progress that we must speak. In his actual remarks on the subject of immortality in *Religion* (p. 149) which include a very curious discussion of the parable of the 'unjust steward' and a characteristically Kantian comment on that of the 'sheep and the goats', he speaks in terms of reward; yet in the concluding sentence (p. 150) he adds significantly

[4] Greene and Hudson, p. 43.

and it became evident that when the Teacher of the Gospel spoke of rewards in the world to come he wished to make them thereby not an incentive to action but merely (as a soul-elevating representation of the consummation of the divine benevolence and wisdom in the guidance of the human race) an object of the purest respect and of the greatest moral approval when reason reviews human destiny in its entirety.

Here for the emphasis on reward something much subtler is substituted, something that coheres with the treatment of grace to which reference has been made earlier in the paper.

(b) In comparison with the three *Critiques*, *Religion* is a comparatively short work; but it is one of considerable complexity in which the author shows a refreshing readiness to modify in his detailed discussions of religion and theological concepts the general principles of his philosophy of religion.

The deep pessimism of his doctrine of 'radical evil' with which the work begins is perhaps its best known contribution to his moral philosophy. In this section it emerges quite clearly that for Kant God is less the creator than the ultimate judge. Thus on p. 66 we read

The extent of his guilt is due not so much to the infinitude of the Supreme Lawgiver whose authority is thereby violated (for we understand nothing of such transcendent relationships of man to the Supreme Being) as to the fact that this moral evil lies in the *disposition* and the maxims in general, in *universal basic principles* rather than in particular transgression. (The case is different before a human court of justice, for such a court attends merely to single offences and therefore to the deed itself and what is relative thereto, and not to the general disposition.)

Nothing is said concerning the manner of this ultimate judge's knowledge of the 'general disposition' of which Kant speaks. It is in the *Critique of Judgment*, in the section in which he discriminates between an intuitive and a discursive understanding,[5] that Kant makes his contribution to the analysis of the metaphysical concept of omniscience. While human understanding involves the use, the refinement, the distinction, the integration of concepts understood as recognitional capacities, in the case of an intuitive understanding, which Kant represents as creating its own objects, those objects are immediately transparent to it. Where such an understanding is concerned, no question arises concerning the identification of an unknown particular, the suitability of this concept or that to this or that situation. Such an understanding never needs to ask what a thing is; it has no need to infer, to question, to guess, to put its view of the particular situation to the test. In human life we are often puzzled by the motives and intentions of those with whom we live; our own behaviour is frequently very far from transparent to us, and we are surprised when we are made to recognize, for instance, that our supposed disinterested kindness was an elaborate essay in unacknowledged self-regard, in which, partly unknown to ourselves, we sought to cut a figure with our fellows. But where an intuitive understanding is concerned, we have to reckon with an understanding that is set free from the sorts of built-in limitations that Kant supposes characteristic of such an understanding as our own. In the *Critique of Judgment* he is not arguing that there *is* in fact such an understanding; he invokes the concept of its activity to complete the account of the rôle of conceptual thinking in human knowledge which he had begun in the Metaphysical Deduction of the categories in his first *Critique*. But in interpreting this passage in *Religion* concerning the 'Supreme Lawgiver', we are perhaps justified in illuminating Kant's meaning by reference to this very interesting passage in the *Critique of Judgment*.

Yet in *Religion* the extreme pessimism of its introduction

[5] Bernard's translation, p.319ff.

prefaces his extended treatment of the traditional Christian theology of redemption by Christ. In these sections of the work one is made aware of Kant's familiarity with the commonplaces of theological argument, especially in the Lutheran tradition with which he was naturally most immediately familiar. Inevitably the argument focuses on the work of Christ and its significance for what Kant describes as the 'conflict of the Good and the Evil principle'. Any suggestion of substitutionary atonement is necessarily alien to his insistence on human autonomy. Yet he seeks to give to Christ's work a significance which goes far beyond that of a classic example of innocent suffering, borne with an exemplary heroism and an altogether undiminished compassion for his fellows, including the agents of his torment. The contradiction in his position is well illustrated by the following long quotation:

> Yet the good principle has descended in mysterious fashion from heaven into humanity not at one particular time alone but from the first beginnings of the human race (as anyone must grant who considers the holiness of this principle, and the incomprehensibility of a union between it and man's sensible nature in the moral predisposition) and it rightfully has in mankind its first dwelling place. And since it made its appearance in an actual human being, as an example to all others [it may be said that] 'he came unto his own, and his own received him not, but as many as received him, to them gave he power to be called the sons of God, even to them that believe in his name'. That is, by example (in and through the moral idea) he opens the portals of freedom to all who, like him, choose to become dead to everything that holds them fettered to life on earth to the detriment of morality; and he gathers together, among them, 'a people for his possession, zealous of good works' and under his sovereignty, while he abandons to their fate all those who prefer moral servitude.
>
> So the moral outcome of the combat, as regards the hero of this story (up to the time of his death), is really not the *conquering*

of the evil principle—for its kingdom still endures, and certainly a new epoch must arrive before it is overthrown—but merely the breaking of its power to hold, against their will, those who have so long been its subjects, because another dominion (for man must be subject to some rule or other), a moral dominion, is now offered them as an asylum where they can find protection for their morality if they wish to forsake the former sovereignty. Furthermore, the evil principle is still designated the prince of this world, where those who adhere to the good principle should always be prepared for physical sufferings, sacrifices, and mortifications of self-love—[tribulations] to be viewed, in this connection, as persecutions by the evil principle, since the latter has rewards in his kingdom only for those who have made earthly well-being their final goal (pp. 77–78).

He goes on to speak of the need of 'divesting' this 'mode of presentation' of its 'mystical veil' in order that its rational sense may be made binding for the whole world. He identifies this sense with the recognition that only the sincerest adoption of genuinely moral principles into their disposition can achieve salvation for men. It is not so much their sensuous nature which works against this adoption as a 'certain self-incurred perversity' which he goes on characteristically to call 'falsity'. He is extremely guarded in what he says concerning Christ's work. Much of his argument inclines him to treat the story of Jesus' ministry and death as a supremely educative illustration of what is possible in spite of the pervasiveness of self-regard and self-deceit in human action. Yet when he speaks, for instance, of 'a moral dominion . . . offered (to men) as an asylum where they can find protection for their morality if they wish to forsake the former sovereignty', he seems to go some way beyond this position, as if the coming of Christ were itself a proleptic vindication of the good man's hope that his stubborn, if often interrupted, effort to purify his motives, to deepen his self-knowledge and free himself in respect of the springs of his action from deep self-deception, is not doomed to frustration. Kant

33

seems to come very near one of the deepest theological insights of the fourth Gospel, namely that Jesus in his rejection, presented by Pilate as one who in his purple robe and crowned with thorns should be too ridiculous for men to bother to compass his destruction, is the ultimate judge of all the world, and that by that judgement, carried out in a setting in which he is identified with those he arraigns, the world is purified.

The passage with which we have just been concerned is followed by a section on miracle, in which Kant devotes some space to criticizing the tradition of allegedly demonic miracles. What he says is closely bound up with his treatment of grace. But he also (p. 81) makes use of his metaphysical agnosticism, seeming to imply that a confident employment of the concept of the miraculous involves a totally invalid supposition that the ways of divine ordering of the world are open to us; whereas they cannot be regarded even as conceivable.

(c) On p. 59 there is a long footnote:

> At this point let me remark incidentally that while, in the ascent from the sensible to the supersensible, it is indeed allowable to *schematize* (that is, to render a concept by the help of an analogy to something sensible), it is on no account permitted us to *infer* (and thus to *extend* our concept), by this analogy, that what holds of the former must also be attributed to the latter. Such an inference is impossible, for the simple reason that it would run *directly counter* to all analogy to conclude that, because we absolutely need a schema to render a concept intelligible to ourselves (to support it with an example), it therefore follows that this schema must necessarily belong to the object itself as its predicate. Thus, I cannot say: I can *make comprehensible* to myself the cause of a plant (or of any organic creature, or indeed of the whole purposive world) only by attributing intelligence to it, on the analogy of the artificer in his relation to his work (say a watch); therefore the cause (of the plant and of the world in general) must itself *possess* intelligence. That is, I cannot say that this postulated intelligence of the cause conditions not merely

my comprehending it but also conditions the possibility of its being a cause. On the contrary, between the relation of a schema to its concept and the relation of this same schema of a concept to the objective fact itself there is no analogy, but rather a mighty chasm, the overleaping of which (*metabasis eis allo genos*) leads at once to anthropomorphism. The proof of this I have given elsewhere.

Kant insists that what he called schematization on no account allows us to suppose ourselves warranted by the analogy we have invoked in finding correspondence in the supersensible to the sensible. He refers to the principles he has established in the *Critique of Judgment* on the use of teleological explanation in biology, where we are entitled to suppose plants in their growth answering to the concept of a pre-formed purpose provided that we recognize the supposition of such an integrating design to be no more than an 'as if' which allows us to treat the plant as a whole.[6] What he says in this passage in the *Religion* shows how deeply he held to the metaphysical agnosticism he had established in his first *Critique*. We must (p. 58) in religion speak of God's love towards the world and we must represent this love in terms of sacrificial self-giving. To suppose that an all-sufficient being could sacrifice a part of what belongs to his state of bliss or rob himself of a possession is to entertain a nonsense. But it is the kind of nonsense which we may safely indulge in once we have resolutely made our own the inescapable limitation of any sort of analogical representation.

By such representation we convey to ourselves nothing whatsoever concerning the ultimate, which for Kant can never be the subject matter of referential or descriptive statement. It is, however, more than an exercise in make-believe; for behind phenomena there lie 'things in themselves', of which indeed we are able to say nothing, but which, by our hardly admissible

---

[6] *Zweckmässigkeit ohne Zweck*

recognition of their reality, compel us again to recognize that which lies beyond the reach of our experience, of which, indeed, if we speak at all, we must speak in an idiom that only recognition both of its sheerly analogical character, and of the essentially unknown structure of that to which it points, authorizes us to use. It is with the tradition of 'negative theology', that in the end Kant, who can neither accept a religious faith that presupposes a divine self-revelation nor completely subordinate the entertainment of its possibility to morality as an instrument that serves the effective extension of the latter's authority, comes to rest. It is indeed his doctrine of the limitations of human experience that provides the background to his vindication of moral freedom, and it is to the same sustained argument that he returns in his tentative attempt to answer the questions relating to the status of religious *credenda*.

In his later writings Kant makes bold and sometimes extremely effective use of analogies. Thus in the *Tugendlehre* Section 24 (Darmstadt edition, 1971, p. 285) he writes:

> Wenn von Pflichtgesetzen (nicht von Naturgesetzen) die Rede ist und zwar im äusseren Verhältnis der Menschen gegen einander, so betrachten wir uns in einer moralischen (intelligibelen) Welt, in welcher, nach der Analogie mit der physisichen, die Verbindunt vernünftiger Wesen (auf Erden) durch Anziehung und Abstossung bewirkt wird. Vermöge des Prinzips der Wechselliebe sind sie angewiesen, sich einander beständig zu nähern, durch das der Achtung, die sie einander schuldig sind, sich im Abstande von einander zu erhalten, und, sollte eine dieser grossen sittlichen/Kräfte sinken:, 'so würde dann das Nichts (der Immoralität) mit aufgesperrtem Schlund der (moralischen) Wesen ganzes Reich, wie einen Tropfen Wasser trinken' (wenn ich mich hier der Worte Hallers, nur in einer andern Beziehung, bedienen darf).

Here Kant uses the complementary attractive and repulsive

action of forces in a Newtonian gravitational field as an analogue of the way in which in human love, those who love one another must avoid in order to preserve the authenticity of their mutual affection, the attempt either to achieve domination over the beloved, or so to be sucked into the beloved's orbit that affection degenerates into an infatuation as destructive to the one who is the object of infatuation as it is to the one who is infatuated. Yet no one reading this passage in Kant's last considerable work on ethics supposes that he thinks his readers will believe that there is any ontologically grounded community between analogatum and analogate.

But in the passage in *Religion* with which we are concerned, the matter is different. There Kant issues his warnings against the transformation of a *schematism of analogy* (one might say, *mere* analogy) into a schematism of *objective* determination (p. 58). He does this partly because he was fully aware that the strange idiom of a divine self-giving had been employed in respect of a particular human life which Kant clearly believed had been lived, and lived in such a way as to invite the sort of commentary, in which by sheer anthropomorphism, the kind of language regarded as appropriate in characterization of the way in which that life was lived (complete spontaneous self-disregard, a readiness to sacrifice all consideration of vindication at the bar of informed contemporary opinion to accessibility to human need and to the claims upon him of the Ultimate to whom alone he regarded himself as accountable; one should recall the importance in the argument of the *Grundlegung* of Kant's comment on the question of Jesus: Why callest thou me good?) is extrapolated to represent the secret of its origin. It belongs to the religious life, as Kant conceives it, that its orientation in the Christian tradition upon the career of an historical individual (including his relentless self-discipline in respect of the springs of his action) encourages a peculiar indulgence in anthropomorphism, as necessary to the proper

37

religious engagement with the realities of moral evil as it is intellectually perilous.

The prophylactic against the destructive consequences of such indulgence is to be found in the paradoxical insistence of the *Critique of Pure Reason* that while we may confidently affirm the necessity of certain structural constants in the world around us, we do so only in respect of a world that is, where its pervasive forms are concerned, conformed to the conditions of our experiencing. Others than Professor Strawson have spoken of Kant's anthropocentrism; but unlike him, they have seen that his distinction between phenomena and 'things-in-themselves' (as well as continuing to a new level of sophistication Locke's distinction between nominal and real essences, so rightly commended by Professor Bennett in his valuable book—*Locke, Berkeley, Hume*[7]) provides him with the means of acknowledging that which it lies beyond our intellectual capacity to represent and with the method at once of measuring up to its intractability, while becoming acclimatized to the peculiar rôle of the idiom by which we seek to indicate it.

It is here that part of the significance of Kant's *Religion* is to be found. There is much in it to which I have not referred; for instance, the lengthy treatment of the relation between religion and clericalism, which while reminding the reader of Kant's sympathy with the temper of the *Aufklärung*, shows a remarkable degree of insight into the peculiar moral problems confronting the religious devotee, impelled by sense of obligation to override the obstacles that seem to him to stand in the way of his would-be convert's adherence to what he regards as supremely precious. In this section Kant's insistence on the subordination of religion to morality is inevitably emphasized;

---

[7] Jonathan Bennett, *Locke, Berkeley, Hume* (pp. 120ff.). It will be realized that I go beyond what Professor Bennett suggests in finding an analogue with Kant's distinction, and indeed in what a strict interpretation of Locke may permit.

but the mood of the work is still set by the emphasis of its opening on 'radical evil' (for Kant an inexplicable reality that must be accepted), and the student of Kant's philosophy will find in it (in a way significantly different from that of the *Metaphysik der Ethik*), whether or not he is interested in its tortuous but extremely interesting treatment of the problems of religious belief, a very significant complement to the self-conscious formalism of the *Grundlegung*, and a continuance of the philosopher's enquiry into the significance of statement concerning the transcendent both tantalizing and suggestive. For the student of the philosophy of religion its elusive fusion of the style of *'theologia negativa'* with a continually renewed plea for the subordination of religion to morality makes it a unique work.

Chapter 3

SOME REFLECTIONS ON TIME AND SPACE

(In Memory of Enrico Castelli)

There is no part of Kant's philosophical work more continually hammered than his treatment of time as a subjective form of inner sense. Elementary students of his development know that this doctrine (and the corresponding doctrine of space), was first presented in bold outline, almost in caricature, in his Inaugural Dissertation of 1770. In the two editions of the *Critique of Pure Reason,* it undergoes considerable modifications; but the philosopher never abandons his underlying commitment to the view that time does not characterize things in themselves. Yet it would be a sheer mistake to attribute to him the metaphysical doctrine that time is unreal, or even that it is simply a construct of human devising.[1] It is not that he does not show himself profoundly sensitive to the role of chronometry in determining the concept of time; the sort of world in which causal lines could not be traced would be one in which human beings would be bereft of any sense of temporal direction, or of an irreversible before and after. Yet what is measured must be there to be measured, even if it is through measurement that it becomes what we take for granted that it is. But what do we mean when we say that it must be there?

Kant's answer is to direct our attention in the first instance to the phenomenology of our sense experience, something which seems, as it were, to provide the spring-board from which our everyday world and the universe, whose remotest bounds we

---

[1] I emphasize later the element of construction in Kant's conception, of a directionally irreversible all-embracing time-order.

seek to reach, alike take off, regarded as objects of experience; and how else, according to Kant, can we take stock of them? There is no other guise under which we can represent to ourselves both their particularities and their constant orders. It is as if he comes to a stop, imposing a profound agnosticism concerning the ultimate status of the temporal as something outside the bounds of our experience.

Of course the imperative to argue in this way issues from Kant's long engagement with the controversy between Newton and Leibniz concerning space and time. This great metaphysical argument is classically presented in the long correspondence between Leibniz and the English divine, Clarke, where the reader is initiated into the arcana of the controversy. Even if he has the 20th century transformations of the concepts of space and time in mind, the reader of these letters finds himself brought sharply up against fundamental questions relating to the status of time and space, of the basic relational order of the world. There is, in the way in which the argument of this correspondence goes, the sort of oscillation between rationalist and empiricist considerations that marks the work of the great philosophers, that is indeed manifestly present in Kant's own writings. Appropriately it is Leibniz who emerges often as the empiricist, challenging his correspondent with the vacuousness of Newton's ideas of an all-embracing infinite plenum, and a uniformly flowing all-embracing river. Yet, for all the surd quality of Newton's conception, in Kant's view it is Newton who fastens correctly on the sheer, almost brute-givenness of space and time. We have to reckon not with the confused presentation of systems of intelligible relations, but with that which is given to us to come to terms with.

So Kant has recourse to his doctrine of space and time as forms of outer and inner sense, and the latter is, of course, the more pervasive of the two; for the flow of human mental activity is temporal, and Kant would seem to believe that such was far from entirely reducible to terms of spatial movements.

It may not be altogether fanciful at this point to recall Augustine's insistence that creation did not take place in time, but that rather time came into being with creation.

We all know that the status of the temporal was a topic on which the author of the *Confessions* often brooded in ways that recalled the Platonism of his intellectual formation, but which at the same time showed (in my judgement) awareness of Aristotle's treatment of time as « the measure of movement ». Yet it was on the manner of the involvement of the temporal with human self-awareness that this great master of intellectual introspection most deeply brooded, as if the secret of the status of the temporal was most nearly captured when the manner of that involvement was laid bare. Augustine's place in the history of philosophy is unquestionably with those who argue from within outwards. Since Gilson, his influence on Descartes has been a commonplace of the schools; the *Cogito* is already there in his writings. But Descartes' critic Pascal, is as much indebted to the same metaphysical tradition as he is to the African doctor in respect of his theology of grace. When he affirms the dignity of the human « thinking reed », in the face of the limitless space of the universe around him, it is to irreducible spiritual experience that he appeals, and in making this appeal he exalts the status of an awareness whose stuff is through and through temporal. This though memory enables the experient to transcend that temporality, even as through his remembering he is enabled to affirm it.

If it is with creation that time comes into being, it is in human experience (or it may be, I should say, through human speech), that that structure of creation takes shape. Yet Kant, who in his genius sought to thread the narrow path between idealism and realism, also qualified this approach which in some respects he shared, in two very important ways. He recognised that in the temporal we had to reckon with that which is sheerly given;

from Newton he came to appreciate the intractable surd element in space and time alike, encouraged of course, where the former was concerned, by his conviction that the Euclidean metric was built-into space, as we had to deal with it. Therefore, although we must be agnostic where « things in themselves » are concerned, we can and must allow an inconceivable correspondence between the ways in which what we experience is temporally and spatially distributed, and the way in which things are. At the level of sense we are passive, and space and time are the forms of this passivity. At least this is their status genetically; but they are also constructs, frameworks through which objectivity is possible, and to realise them as such the passivity of sense must be complemented by the creativity of imagination and understanding. Yet only if through understanding and imagination certain conditions can be realised in our experience, will the unitary irreversible time-order emerge as its most wholly comprehensive context.

The obscurity of this section at least bears witness to the depth at which Kant engaged with the complementarity in our experience of the given and the devised, of the received and the created. If in his own work these problems were stated primarily in epistemological terms, they have a very clear ontological correlate, at which we have already glanced. For Kant self-awareness was unique and irreducible; his doctrine of categories takes for granted that we know from within what it is to understand discursively and can grasp the ways in which that basic act of recognition is inherently diversified. Again, we know what it is to acknowledge the sovereignty of the categorically imperative, and to find in ourselves the necessary conditions under which alone we can significantly speak of its constraint upon us. Yet self-awareness, the presence of the self to itself, is not something that can flourish in a vacuum. The human dimension of the temporal is woven together inextricably with the cosmological. Without the latter the former would elude our grasp: the introspection in which a part of our human dignity is rooted is parasitic upon response to an irreversible exterior order. Memory as we know it, demands constant conditions for its effective reach; if it is creative, its creativity is not absolute. Certainly through recollection we are enabled to create in ways analogous to that in which the artist's spatial perception enables him to realise a quite original « composition » from the elements in the landscape which confronts him. But the memory through which the very substance of our lives *sub specie aeternitatis* is realised, is a memory that is initially fettered to « recall », even as it strenuously seeks in various ways to transcend it. If we say that the significance of a human life is not found in the almost haphazard sequence of events that makes up the series of its biography, yet apart from such a sequence, in which the one event follows the other as does, it is nothing at all. The very creativity of divine grace cannot obliterate the built-in order in which the episodes of a man's life follow the one upon the other.

But do not these reflections take for granted a fixity in the concepts of time and space that recent work in physical theory has shown to be an illusion? On this point my lamentable deficiency in mathematical equipment necessarily compels me to qualify any and every statement that I make. Yet if we begin denying fixity to any concept, we have to ask ourselves what justifies us in grouping together under that concept the various elements we suppose to exemplify it. Since space and time are not universal abstract concepts as, for instance, colour is, we had better speak of spatiality and temporality, and ask ourselves what we suppose all that we regard spatial and temporal to have in common. More narrowly in this part of our inquiry we should ask ourselves what it is that we suppose to warrant our treating as concepts of physical space and time, our vastly transformed understandings of these structures.

Where space is concerned, we have to reckon with the

question whether or not space is endowed with a built-in metric, whether, that is, space is intrinsically Euclidean. The question of the status of geometry and the principles governing the application of geometric systems to the actual world is among the most important raised for the contemporary philosopher, who is genuinely concerned to lay bare the nature of the *a priori*. There is an attractive simplicity in the thought of a Newtonian space given as a whole, with its geometrical structure present as a part of itself. In such a case questions what it is that geometry is applied to, do not arise; the whole problem of congruence is simplified, and the elusive question of the choice of a method of congruence does not have to be raised. Yet the historian knows that Euclid's « parallels' postulate » has been under fire since Proclus, and since the work of Lobachewski and Bolyai, we have been familiar with the reality of alternative geometrical systems. Thus in Euclidean geometry the internal angles of a triangle are equal to two right angles; in hyperbolic geometry they are equal to less than two right angles; in spherical geometry they are equal to more than two right angles. Stellar parallax measurements seem to tell us whether or not the geometry of the rigid body geodesics is Euclidean. But the qualification indicated in use of the word *seem* is quite deliberate. For immediately one recalls the great controversy whether or not the choice is made on empirical grounds, or whether it is conventional in the special sense given to that term by Henri Poincaré, for whom (if I understand his writings at all), the choice of a metric was prescibed by a free choice governed in part, at least, by the theorist's sense of the system of knowledge he was seeking to articulate. Yet, even if Poincaré is wrong, and the theoretician's selection of this or that geometrical system is imposed by the actual observed lay-out of the spatial realities involved, it is still the creativity of the mathematician which provides the method of measurement invoked. In itself that method is a mathematical creation, and the act whereby spatial actualities are brought into relation with its structure demands not only the selection of candidates for congruent interpretation, but the ready availability of the system whereby these candidates are mathematically to be interpreted.

These issues are of the greatest technicality, and although my indebtedness to such works as Professor Adolf Grünbaum's *Philosophical Problems of Space and Time* (2nd enlarged edition, D. Reidel Publishing Co., Dordrecht-Holland/Boston-U.S.A. 1973) can hardly be exaggerated, I have to acknowledge continued technical incapacity to follow the detail of their argument. Why then do I risk making myself ridiculous by entering such territory? I do so because in any sort of philosophical ontology questions relating to the status of space and time are clearly of the greatest importance. But they also touch most intimately on questions relating to the situation of human beings in the world to which they belong. For if we are asked what is fixed in the concepts of the spatial, and the temporal, we find ourselves compelled to answer in crudely psychological terms that they are the most pervasive structural elements in our experience, so that we are defeated in any attempt to imagine an experience that is bereft of their assertive inescapable presence. Here we seem to come back very close to Kant's view of their genetic status. Yet we saw that their pervasiveness, the unimaginability of their absence, demanded that they should be structured. Thus where time is concerned, there must be an objective before and after, and this direction is not something, as it were, given along with time in its bare, inconceivable primitive nakedness, but discerned in and through the tracing of irreversible causal lines in the world of our experience. Yet the brief discussion of the geometrical structure of space has emphasized the extent to which that structure is itself something of which we find it hard to say whether it is discovered or invented. And something of the same kind seems to face us when we come to ask concerning the status of cosmological time.

In the excellent chapter on the causal theory of time in his book, Professor Grünbaum writes as follows: (Op. cit. pp. 293):

> My motivation for advancing below a particular version of the causal theory of time in which the attempt is made to dispense entirely with these psychological deliverances in the axiomatic foundations derives from the following two premises: (a) the thesis of astrophysics (cosmogony) and of the biological theory of human evolution that temporality is a significant feature of the physical world independently of the presence of man's conscious organism and hence might well be explainable as a purely physical attribute of those preponderant regions of space-time which are not inhabited by conscious organisms, and (b) the view of philosophical naturalism that man is part of nature and that those features of his conscious awareness which are held to be isomorphic with or likewise ascribable to the inanimate physical world must therefore be explained by the laws and attributes possessed by that world independently of human consciousness. When coupled with certain results of statistical thermodynamics, the version of the causal theory of temporal order to be advanced below provides a unified account of certain basic features of physical and psychological time. Since man's body participates in those purely physical processes which confer temporality on the inanimate sector of the world and which are elucidated in part by the causal theory of time, that theory contributes to our understanding of some of the traits of psychological time.
>
> So much for the justification of our use of the rudimentary symmetric causal relation as a primitive and of eschewing reliance on the deliverances of psychological time.

In these paragraphs, Professor Grünbaum gives expression with admirable clarity to our sense of time as something that belongs to the natural universe in total independence of the presence in that universe of conscious human subjects, or of the devices (clocks are the most obvious), which they have invented in order to capture its order. There is no doubt at all that Grünbaum is here doing justice to our sense that it is not enough to treat time as subjective, and that the habit so attractive to those whose formation is literary rather than mathematical, of allowing themselves to dwell exclusively on the human dimension of time, is another example of philosophising on the cheap. Yet even if we acknowledge the deadliness of this temptation, and insist on attention to time as a part of nature, we are immediately confronted with the problem of the status of our concept of nature. Is it a concept that is through and through empirical? Or is it the work of our inventive genius? Or has it something of both in its make-up? Is the way in which we suppose the world to be necessarily saturated with our inescapable human perspective upon its processes, even if we admit that a part, at least, of our search for objectivity is constituted by our efforts at elimination of any and every distortion springing from the subtle intrusions of such viewpoints?

In these reflections I have done little more than raise in crude outline some fundamental problems in the theory of knowledge, and indeed in the philosophy of nature, which are of the greatest relevance to the metaphysician, and indeed to the theologian. The latter is only too ready to treat the problems of the relation of the temporal to the eternal as if they could be identified with that of the status of human history. Yet even such restriction compels attention to the problem of the reality of time for God, the extent to which distinctions of before and after, whether in the world of historical change or that of personal biography, obtain for him. Most certainly if anything has been established by these reflections, we have seen that such distinctions are not found in human history, but rather, as it were, brought to the scrutiny of that history from their articulation in the context of elementary human perception. It is with the intensely difficult question of the extent to which this articulation is a fashioning or finding that this essay has been concerned. But whether fashioning or finding, it is what we extrapolate when we come to write of historical change, or even to muse upon the mysteries of personal existence *sub specie aeternitatis*. The epistemological riddles raised by the most elementary and most fundamental cosmology are not dissolved if we suppose it more existentially satisfying to turn to human history, and this is surely seen to be inevitable if we allow ourselves to remember all the time that although our concept of nature is subject to most radical transformation, it remains a concept of nature, and of nature we remain ineluctably a part. Where that nature is concerned, nothing is more fundamental structurally than temporal and spatial order, and the imperative therefore, as far as we can, to grasp their sense is one that it is sheerly frivolous for us to ignore.

Chapter 4

SOME ASPECTS OF THE TREATMENT OF CHRISTIANITY BY THE BRITISH IDEALISTS

It was in December 1868, a little less than fifteen years before his death, that T. H. Green entered into correspondence with the young Henry Scott Holland and R. L. Nettleship (later to be his literary executor) on the occasion of the latter's visit to the young Gerard Manley Hopkins, then on the threshold of entering the novitiate of the Society of Jesus. Part of this correspondence is preserved in Stephen Paget's memoir of Scott Holland,[1] and no student of the interpretation of Christianity in the writings and teachings of the British Idealists should neglect either this exchange of letters, or indeed the later correspondence with Scott Holland in which the young Anglican, on the eve of his own ordination, sought to defend his commitment to his mentor.

The letters are fascinating; for Green is the enemy and powerful critic of any sort of metaphysical naturalism, and from him Holland (and indeed Charles Gore) had learnt lessons in metaphysics and ethics that were to mark their teaching for decades. In Holland's case the rhetoric of many of his sermons as Canon of St Paul's is suffused by the ethical and political ideas of his master in philosophy, and there are continual resonances in his pulpit performance of the ideas posthumously to receive published expression in Green's *Principles of Political Obligation*. Green's influence is also discernible in his well-known hymn: *Judge eternal, throned in splendour.* If Holland stood in the following of the Tractarians, who claimed themselves to be reactivating the Anglican tradition of Laud, Andrewes, Cosin

---

[1] (London: John Murray, 1921): see especially pp. 29–33.

and Wilson, Green taught their liberal-minded *epigoni* to feel at home not only with the idiom of the men of the Putney and Whitechapel debates, but with the arcana of Rousseau's *Contrat Social* itself.

Yet between Holland and his master, there is a great gulf fixed, and in the letters concerned with Hopkins' resolve to put his life at the disposal of the Society of Jesus, the abyss yawns. A twentieth-century student of the Exercises of St Ignatius, R. P. Gaston Fessard S.J. can be fascinated by their anticipation of fundamental Hegelian themes. But it is the dualism implicit in the Jesuit *askēsis* that shocks Green, and seems to him to involve a turning away from the moral demands of the human life around him to a morbid concentration on the *Einmaligkeit* of the supposed self-disclosure of God in Jesus. For Green, though much less explicitly than in Edward Caird's Gifford Lectures on *The Evolution of Religion*, the movement from life to death to resurrection has its place in human existence; but it is a movement profoundly naturalized through transcription into the earthly exchange of self-regarding existence for pursuit of a common good only to receive back (as it were) that self, whose ultimate well-being all human beings must seek, in the transformed and deeply enriched shape of a common life, renewed through the prevalence over individual self-regard, of an all-reconciling common order.

To write in these terms is grossly to oversimplify the range of Green's thought, in particular to omit even an outline of his metaphysical doctrine. Some of the contributors to the symposium: *Lux Mundi*: clearly found this akin to the Logos theology of the Greek fathers. But Gore turned it to interesting account in the rationale he offered of the Eucharistic presence in his subtle, if largely forgotten, contribution to the theology of the Eucharist—*The Body of Christ*.[2] More seriously the

---

[2] (John Murray, 1901): see especially pp. 150–2.

comments made may seem to belittle Green's sense of the energy he believed men continually derived from the Christian religious tradition, which helped to turn them from self-regarding ambition to sense of a common order promoted by their individual efforts, but powerful to subdue to its advance their several personal strivings. In writing on Hopkins' decision to enter the novitiate of the Society of Jesus, Green betrays his impatience in words worth quoting: 'It vexes me to the heart to think of a fine nature being victimized by a system which in my "historic conscience" I hold to be subversive of the Family and the State (the capital letters are Green's own), and which puts the service of an exceptional institution, or the saving of the individual soul, in opposition to loyal service to Society.'

Of course the core of Green's metaphysic, the doctrine of a 'universal mind' (characterized by Mr (later Professor) H. H. Price in lectures on Kant and Hume I attended in Oxford in the Hilary Term of 1934 as an 'excessively immanent God') provides the background for his vexation with Hopkins' commitment to what must seem to his critic a dualism, ontologically as well as morally inadmissible. But it must never be forgotten that Green was a pioneer among Oxford dons in accepting responsibility for the conditions of the City of Oxford. The sense in which the 'last enchantments of the Middle Ages' lingered in the stews of St Ebbe's is highly Pickwickian; if the modern reader finds Green's doctrine of the 'universal mind' totally unplausible, he must not forget that it was in answer to the imperatives that mind seemed to lay upon him that Green plunged into the drab detail of local government. It was not enough to satisfy himself intellectually by the promotion of a new philosophy; he had to undertake the down-to-earth chores of work on the City Council. And as his writings on politics bear witness, for him 'will, not force is the basis of the state'. If men must sometimes 'be forced to be free', this paradox did not constitute a disdainful rejection of Mill's plea for non-interference with the experimentation of the gifted individual, but rather a realistic appraisal of the emptiness of such a freedom for the 'denizen of the London yard', and the intellectual hollowness of an élite, which used such ideas as Mill developed in his *Essay on Liberty* as an excuse for an ultimate human irresponsibility.

Green was arguably before all else, a teacher. The influence of his idiom is traceable not only in the pulpit rhetoric of Henry Scott Holland but, as the German student of the influence of the British Idealists, Dr Klaus Dockhorn has pointed out, in the language of Asquith's Diaries. For all Rousseau's influence upon him, Green never belittled the significance of the executive arm in government. The student of his writings is not likely to be antagonized as later by Bosanquet's doctrine of the 'real will' (as if the historical actuality of the *Machtstaat* enshrined values that commanded a kind of uncritical allegiance by the individual).[3] Yet Green too could write of Bonaparte's bloody progress through Europe as if the dissemination of the principles of the Code Napoléon justified the appalling suffering that the conqueror's advance made inevitable. The delicate humanity which, *malgré tout*, suffuses the writings and speeches of Edmund Burke (not least the sensitivity continually shown to the suffering of the people of his mother's homeland Ireland) is somehow lacking. Green does not offend as Thomas Carlyle does, by a brutish admiration of the exercise of power for its own sake; but the peril to an empirically imaginative political awareness of an underlying metaphysical commitment (especially of one that is immanentist, as Green's was) is discernible in many places in his work.

Yet his writings remain deeply suggestive. He is an idealist in the basic sense of supposing that the speculative, moral,

[3] Bernard Bosanquet, *The Philosophical Theory of the State*, (1st edn) (London: Macmillan, 1899).

aesthetic, and religious life of the individual is something to which that individual enjoys a unique presence. We know from within what it is like to think, to choose, to create, to pray, and no reductionism however sophisticated its method, can deprive us of the understanding of these activities which is ours because we exercise them ourselves. If other-worldly orientated religious activity demands for Green to be reduced to terms other than itself, to terms, that is, of moral and political effort, it remains that such effort is irreducibly unique, and because it is our effort, we know what it is, and what its cost must be, and no argument can invalidate out comprehension of its intricacies. Any suggestion that government can be reduced to terms of a system of public advantage involves a depreciation of the dignity of law-making and administration that those whose daily work is found in such activity, are entitled instantly to repudiate.

So Edward Caird, like Green a man devoted to higher education as he understood it, speaking as a layman from a pulpit he often adorned, said:

> And the truth to which it is leading us in this generation seems above all to be this, that the Christian must not live mainly for another world, and seek to reach purity by escaping from earthly interests and affections: but that the way to selection here and thereafter lies in a deeper understanding of the wonderful world in which we are placed, and a higher conception of all the ties material and spiritual that bind us to our fellow-men.[4]

The best study known to me of the interpretation of Christianity by the British Idealists is the paper on the subject read by the Rev J. S. Boys-Smith to the Oxford Society of Historical Theology in May 1941, and published by him in the

[4] Edward Caird, *Lay Sermons in Balliol College Chapel* (Glasgow: MacLehose, 1907).

Modern Churchman for October of that year.[5] It is an essay of such outstanding excellence that it threatens to render further judgement superfluous. Mr Boys-Smith concentrates on the significance of the Idealists' work for the problem of the historical element in Christianity, becoming acute at the time at which they wrote and taught. It was indeed with the end of the eighteenth century and the beginning of the nineteenth that the division of the centuries B.C./A.D. began to assume a sheerly conventional significance.[6] Of course the changed perspectives made inevitable by geological research were crucial here. But for our purposes it was vital that men and women gradually came to see that the Christian movement was no longer the supreme watershed in human history, but an episode, albeit one of crucial importance. Here, of course, Hegel's *Jugendschriften* (unknown to Edward Caird, most perceptive of British Idealist interpreters of Hegel himself) were crucial. But even before the work of Dilthey and Nohl, there was enough in Hegel to enable men and women to see that for him Christianity was something to be understood, a kind of illustrative epitome, or condensed picture, showing men and women as by a flash of lightning, the principle and the sense of the whole divinely appointed order of the world. Thus they came to see that the ancient scheme—life, life laid down, life received again: Galilee, Jerusalem, Galilee— presents the substance of the moral life, even as it adumbrates the ultimates of being and becoming. If the journey of Jesus from life to death is no longer, as in the view of traditional orthodoxy, the re-creation of the sum of human things entire; if it is relegated to the status of an episode in the last years of the Jewish state—falling somewhere between Pompey's profanation of the Holy of Holies, and the horrors of the sack of Jerusalem, and the desperate heroism of the defenders of Masada—it is still an

---

[5] *The Modern Churchman* (Oct. 1941), pp. 251–73.
[6] It was the late Professor H. A. Hodges who first pointed this out to me.

episode indicative of the very order of the universe, and of the way in which human life should be lived.

But if Boys-Smith is right to see for instance, in Bradley's early essay on *The Presuppositions of Critical History*,[7] a kind of sketch of the later presuppositions of the British Idealists, he is by reason of his own intense preoccupation with the issues of historical particularity inclined to ignore Bradley's own later preoccupation with questions of truth and reality, and their relations to his earlier logical work. It is of course true that the 'axiom of internal relations' has strong bearing on the tendency of the specialist (whether natural scientist or historian) to fasten on the individual state of affairs as if that could be regarded in a sort of splended isolation from its wider context. What Professor R. G. Collingwood denigrated as the 'scissors and paste' model of the historian's work, encouraged a style of historical writing in which the writer seemed to be setting down a catena of facts. His performance suggested that the paradigm of serious historical work was provided by the old-fashioned school text-book, from which the student is encouraged to memorize a series of dates, monarchical dynasties, legislative enactments, judicial decisions, ministerial changes, international tensions, wars, battles, treaties, etc. as if history were compacted of such supposedly various, isolatable items. This admittedly crude caricature made possible clearer perception of the method of the true historian, who seeks always to understand, whatever form that understanding may take, always, however, aware of the importance for its exercise, of active, constructive imagination.

Yet fact has its place in the world of the historian as in nature. Thus the duckbill platypus, a mammal that lays eggs, but suckles its young,[8] violates by its behaviour a well-established

---

[7] F. H. Bradley, *Collective Essays*, I (London: O.U.P. 1935).

[8] I owe this example (as I owe much else) to Professor H. H. Price.

biological classificatory framework. If the Christian movement is only understood for what it is, when we reckon with what it became and the fruits that it bore, as it spread, and transformed itself as well as with its shadowy beginnings, we have to reckon, as best we can, with the detail of those beginnings. In the Galilee and Judaea in which Jesus taught and acted, there were Herodians, Pharisees, Zealots, adherents to the policy of the Temple authorities: and over all there was the Roman presence. And men and women reacted very differently to the Nazarene: Caiaphas, Nicodemus, Mary of Magdala, Zacchaeus, unnamed interrogators. It is matter of fact that they behaved in one way or another, or sometimes in one way, sometimes in another. A fact may be defined as an event or set of events regarded as making a given proposition true or false. To acknowledge the authority of fact in this way, singular, individual, particular, is not to commit oneself to the sophisticated logic of the 'picture theory of the proposition', let alone to seek to treat complex propositions as truth-functions of the 'picture's' supposed one:one correspondence with atomic fact. Beliefs are contextually highly complex; but they are vulnerable, subject to confirmation or refutation. Therein ultimately resides the attraction of the correspondence theory of truth. The proposition: *Snow is white* is true if and only if snow is white. William Laud died on the scaffold if and only if he so met his death by execution.

Yet Caesar's crossing of the Rubicon was not simply the crossing by a named individual of a northern Italian stream.[9] Certainly if he had not on a certain day crossed that stream, the history of the last years of the Roman Republic would have been very different, and Caesar's own end unlikely to have been that which overtook him on the Ides of March, 44 B.C. But the

[9] See Bradley's essay: 'What is the real Julius Caesar?' in *Essays on Truth and Reality* (London: O.U.P. 1914), pp. 409–27.

event to which we refer as Caesar's crossing of the Rubicon was what it was in virtue of the constitutional order of the Roman Republic, and the precise position Caesar occupied in 49 B.C. Nor would the Caesar who so crossed the Rubicon have been what he was, nor his crossing what it was, but for his rivalry with Pompey and the latter's position and powers at that time. Sooner or later the massive Gallic victories of the pro-consul must receive reference: so too the accommodation achieved at the conference at Lucca, and more remotely, Caesar's blood relationship with Caius Marius, are relevant to the historian seeking to decipher the significance of that moment of supreme crisis.

So the 'axiom of internal relations' inevitably finds mention if only that without it, for the idealist the individual forfeits the uniqueness that makes him what he is. Certainly the considerations that now engage us belong to the philosophy of logic rather than of religion. But who or what is Jesus Christ? The 'quest for the historical Jesus' inevitably engages with his Judaean/Galilean *Sitz im Leben*; but who is that who he is? Is he what he is apart from his relationship not only to Peter, James, John, Judas, Caiaphas, Pilate and the rest, but to others unborn when he was nailed to the Cross, to Ignatius of Antioch, Origen, Arius, Anselm, John Knox, Mother Julian of Norwich, San Carlo Borromeo, Lancelot Andrewes, Immanuel Kant, Vladimir Lenin, Menachem Begin, Jerry Falwell and the men and women of the 'moral majority'? Where should one stop, and how discriminate?

The 'axiom of internal relations' belongs to the philosophy of logic rather than to *Religionsphilosophie*. But Caird invoked it powerfully in one of his sermons in Balliol College Chapel, when he claimed 'No absolute differences or antagonisms in the intelligible world, no distinctions which do not imply relations, and therefore an ultimate unity between the things designated'. Caird's monism was unquestioned; and in another place, he extrapolates this same love of unity at all costs in language that recalls Bosanquet's panegyric of the state. 'The national state is still the highest organised whole, the great ethical unity to which our services are immediately owing, and it is in which our services acting with it, or upon it that we can serve humanity.' Later referring to Thucydides and Sophocles he claims, 'When our country is strong, we are uplifted by it.'[10]

Yet Caird, as his attitude to the Boer War shows (and indeed paradoxically Bosanquet's own also) was no exponent of the *Machtstaat* as a law to itself. It was as if with Green, he would find in service of the State, for which he trained men at Balliol through the school of Literae Humaniores, a transcript into nineteenth- and twentieth-century mundane terms of the membership of the Corpus Christi Mysticum, to whose service, in its traditional forms, the Hopkinses of this world, in their seemingly foolish asceticism, offered their lives. But the monism of the idealists remained a perpetually integrating focus of their dedication: a monism whose sources were logical and mystical at the same time, deepening their critical perceptions while it also ensured that self-sacrifice in conduct meant rediscovery of an authentic individuality (transcending the narrow limits of the Aristotelian tradition), and that under the sovereignty of an all-embracing unity, where differences were wonderfully elided, contradictions overcome, and contingency obliterated in a necessity far more than mere causal order, totally satisfying to the most exacting demands of thought and understanding.

It is a commonplace for contemporary political scientists (e.g. Professor S. E. Finer) to identify the common good in practice with the Utilitarian 'greatest happiness of the greatest number'. But the former seemed to the idealist the concrete universal that endowed its manifold particularizations with the authentic spiritual quality of its wholeness: while the latter suggested a

---

[10] *Lay Sermons in Balliol College Chapel* (Glasgow: MacLehose, 1907).

device of almost mechanical contrivance, aimed at providing an increase in allegedly homogeneous human happiness, or at least a *pis aller* enabling individuals to enjoy a modicum of material well-being. The concept of the common good was in the end metaphysical.

It is of course a fallacy to speak here of effort or striving. The 'axiom of internal relations' was in principle deterministic. The very notion of contingency was disbarred; for what an individual became by seeming accident of juxtaposition was essential to its being what it was. What men and women seemed to enjoy by the changes and chances of their day-to-day experiences touched the very substance not only of their individual existence, but of the society they helped to shape. Of course Bosanquet emphasized that a society embodied the 'operative criticism of its own institutions'; but this criticism was mediated 'not by resolute scrutiny of its political and social defects, but by the seemingly accidental intrusion on its own history of the biographies of its citizens'.[11] The society was an organic unit, and the state which promoted and incarnated its wholeness was no device of its ingenious devising, but rather the place at which its history achieved self-conscious definition.

We are in fact faced with a spiritualistic determinism. Certainly to those who rebelled against some of the Benthamite elements, in John Stuart Mill's inheritance, the emphasis on the creative role of the human spirit was liberating; but this role was only in a very subordinate sense creative; for it was in fact the agent of a collective spiritual unity, sovereign in all its doings, and oblivious (seemingly) of the tragic destiny of the individual. In no writer does this emphasis in the sovereignty of the all-embracing spiritual whole receive clearer or more powerful

[11] Bosanquet mentions Themistocles' intervention in respect of the use made of the resources of the silver mines at Laureion by the Athenians.

expression than in the work of Professor Brand Blanshard, in whose voluminous writings the concept of the all-embracing, wholly satisfying, intellectually and spiritually transparent whole achieves perhaps its most effective late twentieth century articulation.

In 1924 Bishop Edward S. Talbot, the first Warden of Keble College, Oxford, and an active associate with Charles Gore in the volume *Lux Mundi*, published an interesting essay[12] on his early life, when as an undergraduate reading history at Christ Church, Oxford, in the middle of the nineteenth century, he was made aware of the commanding influence of John Stuart Mill, both in ethics and politics, and in logic. Although Edward Caird was already teaching at Merton College, and 'Green was showing over the horizon', it was Mill who dominated the world of philosophy. And although Mill was in a certain sense a theist, Talbot claimed that his intellectual ascendancy imposed on those of religious commitment who were sensitive to philosophical issues, a 'two pockets system', with their faith in one pocket and their philosophy in another. It was to Talbot's world that the idealists spoke, *suggesting* a reconciliation between the claims of philosophy and of faith. This lay primarily in their insistence that the life of the mind was transparent to itself, impatient of any sort of translation into terms other than its own which was supremely significant. It could be claimed that in the eighteenth century, Berkeley with his carefully argued distinction between 'ideas' and 'notions' had made this point with admirable clarity in the very context of British empiricism. Indeed it might be further argued that a critical reader could extract from his writings not only an anticipation of Mill's conception of physical objects as 'permanent possibilities of sensation', but a very subtle

[12] E. S. Talbot, *Memories of Early Life* (London: Mowbray, 1st impression 1924), see especially pp. 42–5.

epistemological argument for theism.[13] Again there was Butler, profoundly influential on the young Newman, and not without deep effect on the young Robert Wilberforce, to Gladstone 'our Athanasius'. But Newman had submitted to Rome in 1845, to be followed later by Manning and Wilberforce, and Butler was perhaps in consequence suspect. Further the importance of teleological considerations in Butler's scheme left him *prima facie* vulnerable to the first impact of Darwin's *Origin of Species* in 1859. So it was Caird[14] and Green who liberated the men of the post-Tractarian generation from their intellectual insecurity, and the latter in particular who gave to their political thought, a vitality that was sadly lacking in the years when their loyalties seemed too tightly fettered to the memory of the Caroline divines, for whom 'the divine right of Kings' (I am thinking particularly of Lancelot Andrewes) seemed an element of their fundamental theology.

Yet as Boys-Smith pointed out in his masterly essay, the idealists' understanding of history made them uneasy bed-fellows for those who like Gore and Scott-Holland were committed to a theology of the Incarnation, which, while shocking many traditionalists by its espousal of Kenotic conceptions, was in fundamental intention orthodox. The formulations achieved at Nicaea and at Chalcedon remained for them decisive not only in respect of Christ's person, but in respect of the very grounds of the world's relation to its creator. A study of Scott-Holland's sermons at St Paul's throws into

[13] It may be thought that this was done in the light of Kant's philosophy by H. W. B. Joseph in his Henrietta Herz Lecture: A comparison of the idealism of Kant with that of Berkeley, in *Essays in Ancient and Modern Philosophy* (London: O.U.P. 1935).

[14] Caird's lectures as Professor of Moral Philosophy at Glasgow deeply moved the young Cosmo Gordon Lang in his period as a student there and it was to Caird's memory that William Temple in 1934 inscribed his Gifford Lectures *Nature, Man and God* (London: Macmillan).

THE BRITISH IDEALISTS

clear relief, the tension, even the contradiction, between the details of his Christology and soteriology and the assumptions of his social philosophy. Moreover the idealists were metaphysical logicians, and this aspect of their work remains crucially important.

Professor Nicholas Rescher's[15] recent book—*The Coherence Theory of Truth*—has helped promote a revival of interest in that conception of truth, emancipated from the 'axiom of internal relations' with which it had been closely bound in its formulation, e.g. by F. H. Bradley and H. H. Joachim. Russell in an essay explicitly aimed at Joachim's book—*The Nature of Truth*— and entitled—*The Monistic Conception of Truth*[16] directs his criticism at the ontological conception of the status of relations which be believed to underlie Joachim's doctrine. The confusions involved in this conception were later the target of one of G. E. Moore's most influential papers—*Internal and External Relations*,[17] in which he probed the concept of individuality involved in the theory. Yet coherence as a criterion of truth (if not its nature) remained highly influential, long before such works as Rescher's revivified the theory.

Professor Christopher Longuet-Higgins, F.R.S., pointed out to me in discussion twenty years ago that Christ's alleged changing of water into wine at the wedding-feast of Cana of Galilee necessarily involves a violation of the principle of Dalton's Atomic Theory on which the whole (Professor Longuet-Higgins was emphatic here) of chemistry is founded. The basic postulates of the theory are that ordinary (i.e. terrestrial) matter is composed of atoms of distinct kinds, and that though these atoms may be—and are combined—in different ways to form different substances, the atoms are

---

[15] (London: O.U.P. 1973.)
[16] Bertrand Russell, *Philosophical Essays* (London: Allen & Unwin).
[17] *Philosophical Studies* (London: Routledge & Kegan Paul, 1920).

63

themselves indestructible, and that atoms of one kind cannot be changed into atoms of another. Wine contains, among other ingredients, ethyl alcohol, formula C_2H_5OH, and for water to be changed into wine would violate Dalton's law. Alcohol contains carbon atoms, and the change of hydrogen atoms or oxygen atoms into carbon atoms by any chemical process is no more feasible than the changing of lead into gold atoms.

The language may suggest that of Professor William van Orme Quine in its seeming indifference to the distinction between logical and natural necessity. But the argument is stressing the sheer incoherence of the alleged miraculous occurrence with acknowledged natural laws, and in fact ruling out the claim that the event in question happened on the grounds of that incoherence. The example is valuable as illuminating the sense of the term—*incoherence*—in which incoherence is admitted as ground for rejecting a factual claim. What is rejected is an allegedly unique event that transgresses (to speak metaphorically) an established, internally coherent, and also comprehensive system. One is reminded of the logic of Bernard Bosanquet's *Implication and Linear Inference*,[18] and the role in that essay of the notion of system. The term 'system' is ambiguous; but in the example Longuet-Higgins offers its force is totally clear, and its power to disqualify as outrageous a particular factual claim immediately evident.

For Christianity there is no escape from the unique, whatever view is taken of the factual truth of individual miracle stories. There is the ultimate uniqueness of Jesus of Nazareth; but there is also the 'transcendence of pre-formed character' emphasized in the many discussions of moral freedom to be found in the writings of the late Professor C. A. Campbell.[19] He was himself

[18] (London: Macmillan, 1918). Professor C. D. Broad's critical notice of this book in *Mind* for that year should also be studied.

[19] Some of the most important of these papers are conveniently available in his collection: *In Defence of Freewill* (London: Allen & Unwin, 1968).

a passionate advocate of the idealist conception of judgement; yet he was an even more convinced defender of the individual's power to transcend in action inherited bias, and to reveal himself as the originative author of what he did. For him (as for Kant whose writings he strangely neglects) moral creativity was the very essence of human uniqueness. He took the moral struggle with the utmost seriousness, and showed a kind of obstinate simplicity in the face of every attempt made not least by those with whom he was in considerable sympathy to reduce that struggle to terms of something other than itself. For him the authentic substance of our humanity was disclosed to us in our conviction that e.g. on occasion we should have, and could have, acted otherwise than we did. Nothing would reveal more clearly how great differences obtain between philosophers of generally idealist commitment than development of the contrasts between the work of Professor Campbell and that of Professor Brand Blanshard, two convinced continuators of that philosophical tradition.

Of course Campbell was a Bradleian, and therefore less beholden than other idealists to the kind of ideal of systematic interconnection that dominated Bernard Bosanquet's logical thought. But to remember his work on Maundy Thursday (when this paper was written) is inevitably to be reminded of a man's supreme struggle with himself, and to appreciate the passionate rigour with which one recent idealist philosopher asserted the irreducible actuality of a man's wrestling with himself.[20]

The problem of determinism remains pivotal for the idealist tradition in philosophy in general, and for its interpretation of

---

Attention should also be paid to the papers on this topic of Professor A. E. Taylor, e.g. in his contribution to *Contemporary British Philosophy*.

[20] Campbell's work is certainly exempt from the sort of theological criticism brought against the idealist tradition by P. T. Forsyth in his powerful essay in theodicy, *The Justification of God* (London: Duckworth, 1916).

65

Christianity in particular. It may be fitting to end this somewhat sprawling essay (little more perhaps that a footnote to Boys-Smith's study) with some characteristically paradoxical words of Bradley's:

> Unless the Reality itself enters into the process of events, unless it itself is what it becomes there, unless it itself discovers itself to itself and us, and it takes on a change from that discovery—the Reality itself remains outside knowledge, and itself is unreal. On the other hand, if that which is discovered is not found, if that which appears is not revealed, if in short the thing, which we get to see, was not really there—then reality and knowledge, are once more an illusion. But we are unable to combine these partial truths so as to understand how both of them go to make up the Universe. (Some aspects of truth. In *Essays in Truth and Reality*, p. 337.)

APPENDIX

It remains surprising that the British idealists paid comparatively little attention to Kant. There is Edward Caird's monumental study;[21] there is also (for instance, in Green) a continued sense of indebtedness to the Königsberg philosopher for the weight he laid on self-consciousness as unique and irreducible. But the radical critic of speculative metaphysics, and the subtle exponent of the doctrine of the primacy of the practical reason remains almost unnoticed.

It was in 1926 that Professor C. C. J. Webb (once Brand Blanshard's tutor) published a major study of *Kant's Philosophy of Religion*.[22] But with the notable exception of his significant

---

[21] (Glasgow, 1899: 2 vols.) But Caird for all his scholarship saw Kant as the morning star (faintly glimmering) of the Hegelian dawn.

[22] (London; O.U.P. 1926.) Webb was also H. W. B. Joseph's brother-in-law.

study of the conditions of 'perpetual peace', the opuscula in which Kant draws out some of the implications of his patiently argued *Religionsphilosophie* have only comparatively recently begun to receive the attention they have deserved. The chapter on Kant in Hans Urs von Balthasar's *Prometheus* (published in 1939) was followed in the post-war years by such excellent books as J. L. Bruch's *La Philosophie Réligieuse de Kant*[23] and Dr Michael Despland's *Kant on History and Religion* (the latter containing a translation of Kant's late essay in criticism of all forms of theodicy).[24]

Kant is seen, especially now that his vast superiority as a *religious* thinker to the monumentally tedious and ultimately second-rate Albrecht Ritschl is clear, as a contributor to the philosophy of religion of a quite unusual sensitivity and subtlety. The very contradictions in his later writings on these topics show that sense of the irreducibility of the spiritual (a lesson that he taught in his own terms in the Transcendental Deduction of the Categories, and sought to protect against misconstruction in the Paralogisms of Pure Reason, going on to amplify his teaching by his doctrine of the primacy of the practical reason, and complement it by his subtle theory of teleological judgement) most certainly did not leave him the prisoner of an all-embracing monism. At the same time through the rigour of his criticism of metaphysics, he suggested ways in which the mystery of human transcendence might be received without submission to the crudities of an ill-disciplined anthropomorphism. To write in these terms is not to suggest that in Kant we find solution of our problems, only that in his curiously and carefully nuanced agnosticism we find the road less inadequately to state at least some of them. A dialogue between his point of view and that developed by Professor

[23] (Paris: Aubier, 1970.)
[24] (Montreal: McGill-Queen's U.P. 1973.)

Brand Blanshard in the long series of writings his study of *The Nature of Thought*[25] introduced in 1940, could only prove highly illuminating.

[25] (London: Allen & Unwin, 1940.)

Chapter 5

METAPHOR IN THEOLOGY

It is very important to distinguish two questions, namely the delimitation of the frontiers of the literal and the metaphorical on the one hand, and the issue of the referential character of theological and religious statements on the other. These questions are related; but they are at bottom distinguishable. Even if literal and metaphorical are found to be so closely interwoven that it is a waste of time to try to separate them, this recognition does not condemn the expressions in which they are found to be so interwoven to the status referentially regarded, of a kind of second-best. Further, it is clear that without access to such expressions in which literal and metaphorical terms interpenetrate, one is doomed to an aphasia in which even one's considered rejection of religious or metaphysical claims is rendered futile or empty of significance.

Suppose I speak of the unbridgeable gulf between God and men, between the One whose ways are not as his creation's, and that creation's broodings and aspirations. In so speaking, I am advertising a predicament that can only be conveyed by use of a spatial metaphor. The futility of so much confident speech concerning the ultimate, the very vindication of the indispensable role of silence *in rebus divinis* is something that only the thrust of a recognizable family of metaphorical expressions can convey. If we are to be plunged into silence before the *Deus absconditus*, that silence only overtakes us as we have affirmed his hiddenness: and in that affirmation we are using a metaphor. For God is not hidden as a treasure may be thought hidden, or a valuable that we would protect from a burglar, or even the formula of a drug that will benefit the arthritic without side-effects, sought unremittingly by medical researchers. We have not here to reckon with a hiddenness that will be replaced by discovery. Or if as, say, with the late Professor C. C. J. Webb[1] that we must await God's self-revelation, abandoning a search for him that would diminish his status to that of a Diana on whose privacy an Actaeon could intrude, or a Zeus whose secrets a Prometheus could wrest at will, we are still moving at the level of inexpungable metaphor. For divine self-revelation is something that we schematize to ourselves in terms of an unveiling. But God does not unveil himself as, for instance, the priest unveils the crucifix for veneration in the solemnity of the ancient liturgy of Good Friday. If we use the term unveiling as we must, we are still bound to metaphor; for what we refer to by the idiom of divine self-disclosure is no self-disclosure of a sort known among men.

Yet at this very elementary level, we are bound to make play with metaphors; for we have no other tool with which to convey to ourselves not only the manner of our religious experience (if any), but also our agnosticism. We know what it is to be provided with evidence whether in the laboratory, or the library, in geological field-work, in archaeological research, in criminal investigation. We know also what it is to argue whether or not we have evidence for this or that belief. For instance, New Testament scholars debate whether or not we have evidence that Jesus claimed to be Messiah. There are those who insist that the evidence admits no other conclusion, albeit demanding that we find the notion transformed by his application of it to his own person and work; there are those who judge that the weight of evidence is against such a conclusion; and there are those who maintain the evidence non-supportive either way. These are issues of historical credibility, no different from those confronting the historian of the

[1] See Webb's still valuable early work—*Problems in the Relation of God and Men.*

70

Athenian Empire who seeks accurately to identify the plague that so damaged Athenian will to assist Sparta during the Archidamian war. Certainly the Gospels represent a very different literary form from that exemplified, for example, by Thucydides' *History of the Peloponnesian War* or indeed by Plutarch's *Life of Pericles*. But we may concede that they are (St John as much at St Mark) in some sense intended as historically referential. But when we say that we lack decisive evidence for the existence of God, what are we saying?

Analogy with the other sorts of evidence here mentioned may rightly be insisted; but suppose we go on to ask (a familiar question), what would constitute evidence for his existence. Can we conceive imaginatively the sort of self-authentication which would (if I may speak carelessly) measure up to his authenticity? Anyone recalling here the horrors of Auschwitz could rightly charge me with academic frivolity; for it requires little effort of imagination to conceive the sort of divine intervention in wrath and mercy which to the victims of that unspeakable place would have certified that God had indeed 'rent the heavens and come down'. But because there was notoriously no such intervention nor seemingly (in spite of the ceaseless efforts of such men as Churchill himself) even the merest token challenge to such citadels of Nazi atrocity, are we saying that there was evidence provided there that the description of an almighty who loves justice and mercy is without application? Or did the continuing Jewish fidelity to the covenant, sustained in the midst of horror, provide itself all the evidence that is needed? Is there evidence in the fact that in spite of Nazi wickedness and large-scale Christian acquiesence, the Jews there continued to believe, and the *occasional* Christian (for instance the Carmelite philosopher, Edith Stein, who by reason of birth, died with the ancient people of Yahweh, in whose company she had in some sense, sought to remain)? But for what do such mysteries (in Gabriel Marcel's sense) of faith provide evidence? Do they certify anything other than their own intense reality, that men and women have found in such belief resources great enough to allow their personal, interior triumph (again how am I using the word?) over Hitler's willing agents? Or suppose I say that such fidelity is stronger evidence (stronger because less inappropriate to the object of confession) than could be provided by the literal, i.e. observable, fulfilment of the entreaties of psalmist and prophet? But if I speak so, how am I using the term evidence? Analogy in the sense of something more than metaphor? The frontiers between the two are (strict Aristotelian-style ontology apart) blurred and ill-defined.

We must surely recognize how much of our religious discourse is saturated with a metaphorical groping, and this limitation (if limitation indeed it be) extends to many of our attempts to improve our theological method. For instance, it is often claimed today that in Christology we do best (or least inadequately) if we proceed from 'below upwards' and not from 'above downwards'. We have, of course, all of us been made to reckon with the mythological taint of such language; yet we use it (*faute de mieux*) in the intellectually sophisticated characterization of our methodology. Further, we can go on to criticize the alleged opposition of the two styles on the grounds that their sharp contrast blurs the interpenetration of movement from the familiar to the transcendent and from intimation of the latter to the sheerly earthly. Thus Peter, James and John are witnesses of the communion of Father and Son, seemingly made visible in the passing glories of Mt. Hermon, and also in sharp awareness punctuating their exhausted sleep, of seemingly very different (even pitifully human) aspects of that mysterious union in Gethsemane. In the latter place, hearing (of the five senses empirically shown to be the most resistant to anaesthesia, whether the natural anaesthesia of sleep, or the induced forms employed in modern medicine) plays a more significant rôle than sight, and arguably what there breaks on the apostles' rest, is less easily intelligible than the supposed authentication of Jesus on the mountain, where they saw Moses and Elijah speak with Him.[2] So we may say we need the most assuredly transient *seeming* revelation of the transcendent, to be sharply brought up against its impenetrable mystery. But I say: *seeming* revelation; for the transcendent is that which lies beyond revelation in any schematizable sense. If we think of the mount of transfiguration as the place (and the time) of revelation, we domesticate the concept, making it something made to our measure, forgetting not only the lesson of Gethsemane but that conveyed by the failure to meet immediate human need at the mountain's base. Yet we require the momentary, passing glimpse that Hermon offers to allow the problem of Jesus to be set to us. Problem? Would not Gabriel Marcel have bidden us speak rather of the mystery to be presented for our pondering? But what are we to say of such pondering and its logic and of the categories through which it is articulated?

Here the role of ontology in the classical sense, defined by Professor Peter Geach, as the sustained attempt to provide a systematic account of the concepts used in discussion concerning any subject-matter cannot be underestimated: (such concepts as thing, existence, causality, etc.) It was by means of ontological concepts, and in particular substance, essence, nature that the *mysterium Christi* was classically articulated. But when in the so-called 'Nicene Creed' Jesus is acclaimed as *homoousios* with the Father, it is as if we strip what we are saying of any import that will suggest the manner of this ineffable sharing of Godhead; it is as if we would as near as possible totally formalize the sense of the ascription. But what of the sharing? Here we seem back in

---

[2] It is important to remember that in Luke's version Moses and Elias speak with Jesus of the *exodus* he will accomplish at Jerusalem. On this see the very interesting comment by the poet Dr Geoffrey Hill in his essay on *The Absolute Reasonableness of Robert Southwell* in *The Lords of Limit* (André Deutsch, 1984).

the world of metaphor, of metaphor classically evaluated in its metaphysical use, by Plato's discussion of the relatedness of particulars to Forms in the first part of the *Parmenides*. But the sharing of Godhead between the allegedly equally divine is a communion more esoteric than the one which elicited Plato's criticism of the exposition of his own theory. We need, of course, to turn to the essentially dramatic style of the Gospels (Luke as well as John) to convey to ourselves the manner of that to which we refer when we speak of sharing in such a context.[3] But if we use the term, or abide by its use, to characterize what we find there, a sharing with the Father in the Spirit, a sharing with Christ's brethren, then we oscillate between the highly, elusively metaphorical, and the literal; for after all Jesus (if such a man lived) shared food with family and friends as we do. Yet this sharing is itself represented as part of the meat of obedience by which he lived: and here metaphor comes full tide, and not only in the use of the language of food, but also in use of that of obedience. For obedience is highly ambivalent: never in itself humanly a form of virtue, occasionally allowable as an excuse (e.g. for service in the Wehrmacht from 1939–45). We must never forget that there were those who said No, for instance, the enigmatic Austrian sacristan, Jägerstätter. Yet we say that Jesus obeyed, and go on to characterize, even to mitigate the sense of that obedience, by speaking of it (*obscurum per obscurius*) as an aspect of his transparency to his Father, and his Father's presence in Him. Yet this metaphor of transparency (eloquent in its suggestion) is an awkward, verbal bed-fellow with the more ontologically weighted term, presence, even with the more flexible alternative indwelling.

But the time has come to return to the issue raised at the outset

[3] I have discussed Luke's treatment of the Temptation narrative in my contribution to the volume—*Religious Imagination*, edited by Professor J. P. MacKay (Edinburgh University Press, 1986), and venture to refer the reader to what I have written there concerning its deep Trinitarian sense.

of this paper, of the relation of metaphorical and referential. A very good deal of the preceding material, arguing the saturation of our religious and theological speech by the consciously or unconsciously metaphorical, is perfectly compatible with the allowance that such speech is intentionally referential. It is not simply a matter of the believer's imaginative self-projection; it is (to use an admittedly metaphorical term, already employed in this paper) a groping, a *tâtonnement*: or one is seeking to find one's way, to establish a sense of direction. And one is certainly travelling in order to arrive, seeking to establish a goal towards which to orientate oneself. The transitivity, the other-regarding nature of the activity, is clear: the epistemic realism shows itself. Illusion it may prove in the end to be; but if it does, it will prove itself so, because we seek by our sometimes deliberate, sometimes hardly noticed, verbal innovation to approach the frontiers of the ultimate, the unknown, though supposedly (and this supposition undergirds our effort) not finally unknowable.

Yet, there are many other questions that must be faced: for instance, most importantly, the relation of religion and poetry, a topic beyond the scope of this very tentative paper, but one whose profound relevance must be advertised. But one issue must be mentioned and illustrated, and that of the conditions under which a metaphor may go stale,[4] or alternatively survive, when the conditions of its active use are gone, or indeed still survive in spite of the near-total discarding of those conditions. And here (drawing on the excellent discussion of the issues involved between Fr Fergus Kerr O.P. and Professor Michael Dummett in *New Blackfriars* in 1977), I wish to raise the example of Crucifixion–Resurrection.

Kerr had rightly pointed out that in the tradition of Christ's alleged resurrection, we have to reckon with the presence of

[4] A fine example of the re-vivification of a stale metaphor may be found in Professor Douglas MacMillan's *The Lord our Shepherd* (Evangelical Press of Wales, 1984).

profoundly evocative interpretative elements: for instance the very phrase 'the third day' is one which for any one familiar with the Scriptures of the Old Testament is certainly 'loaded'. It speaks of much more than the mere passage of thirty-six hours. But if Kerr is right here (and I heard similar views put forward by the very conservative scholar, Henry Leighton Goudge, in Oxford in the early months of 1933), Dummett is right to suspect him of moving towards a position which would treat crucifixion–resurrection as nothing more than the characterization of a way of life, the way of apostolic existence traced with unforgettable poignancy by Paul in his *apologia pro vita sua*, the second letter to the Corinthians. Dummett very properly asks Kerr whether in fact such sustained self-interpretation, offered admittedly in self-defence, but reaching in the process an awareness of the inwardness of apostolate, perhaps unequalled in Christian literature, would have 'got off the ground' (the phrase is mine), apart from Paul's belief that the Father raised Jesus from the dead. It is not that it is logically impossible for the metaphor to survive as a metaphor apart from this belief; again it is clearly possible that the usage 'got off the ground' partly, even chiefly in virtue of the Apostle's belief that an event had happened, which as a matter of fact, did not happen. But while it is logically possible for the usage to survive the decline, even disappearance, of the belief in question, such survival would be the survival of a use markedly different from the Apostle's. His language e.g. 'as dying and behold we live' is clearly metaphorical; but for him its power as metaphor is parasitic on a belief whose articulation itself involved metaphor (the term *raised* uneasily threads the frontiers of the literal and metaphorical, but undoubtedly plunges into the latter), but whose content was for Paul, unquestionably factual. It is now suggested (i.e. I am referring to writing later in date than the discussion referred to) that Christianity may indeed dispense with its alleged historical basis: dispense, that is absolutely, and not allow that basis to be reduced to a bare minimum, (the position sometimes defended with great subtlety, by Rudolf Bultmann). Certainly, (and this point is made obliquely by Kerr) the sense of such terms as fact and event, when they are used in respect of Christ's alleged resurrection, requires most careful elucidation; they are certainly being 'stretched' in being used in respect of that which is, if actual, sheerly unique. But Dummett seems to make his point with great force, namely the extent to which a whole array of metaphors demands for its significant employment, a context of belief concerning what has actually happened. This though he should concede that that actuality itself may only be conveyed to us by a language which deliberately goes beyond that of bare factual report. Yet embedded in such discourse is reference to that which is unquestionably a matter of such report. A sequel to this paper (if one were ever to be written) must certainly concern itself with analysis of the notion of fact.

Chapter 6

REFLECTIONS ON MORTALITY

There are few sentences in Wittgenstein's *Tractatus* more often quoted than

'Das Tod ist kein Ereignis
des Lebens; den Tod erlebt Man night'

According to Dr Gershon Weiler,[1] the late Professor Gilbert Ryle suggested that these words should be translated—'Death is not an event of life. Death is not experienced.'

What belongs to an individual's life, the events making up his or her biography, can be remembered or anticipated. We can claim to recall what it was like first to go to school; our claim may be mistaken in as much as the passage of the years may have blurred the poignancy of those far-off days, or even endowed with a spurious delight what was at the time we lived through it (erlebt), very much an ordeal. Again we may ask what it would be like to retire; or more modestly perhaps we say that we cannot imagine what it will be like for our work in the world at large to be finished and for us to be 'on the shelf', (the language is metaphorical). Yet our deliberate and prudent modesty is qualified. We know what it is that we refer to, what, in fact, it is to cease to be professionally employed. We can give cash value to the difference between such a state and that of an unemployment imposed by the economic circumstance of Thatcher's Britain, or a prolonged interruption of normal activity due to serious illness. Moreover, indeed, we can go on giving examples of experiences more and more remote from our own

[1] *Wittgenstein and his impact on contemporary thought*, ed. Holder et al. (Vienna, 1978) pp. 502ff.

imaginative reach. Thus we are often reminded today how the tremendous technological changes of the last century, which provide so much of the accepted context of our daily lives, at the same time render the day-to-day lives of those of earlier generations opaque to our understanding. This so-called 'cultural gap', sometimes greatly exaggerated, is an unquestioned reality; yet the capacity of historians imaginatively to enter into the minds of the men and women whose works and ways they seek to explore, gives the lie to claimants of an unbridgeable gulf (between,) for instance, the world of late republican Rome and our own. And what is certainly the case for the trained historian is also frequently experienced in respect of the moral perceptions and perplexities of men and women long dead, by many of their successors, quite unschooled in the characteristic disciplines of technical historical study. In an age in which political assassination is a relatively common occurrence, the profound reflections, mediated by William Shakespeare's presentation of the murder of Julius Caesar, are assimilable, even if it is the case that the age of Elizabeth Tudor is nearer that of Plutarch (Shakespeare's source), than our own.

We could go on more or less indefinitely adducing any and every sort of extension, indeed transformation, of the world of our every-day experience. We could, if so inclined, and suitably equipped, indulge in fantasies far beyond the reach of the most sophisticated practitioner of 'science fiction'. But we would not by any such exercise reach beyond the frontiers of that which is at least in principle imaginable. Yet death lies beyond all such frontiers.

A man's death is certainly an event in that it has a date, a place in the time-order, simultaneous with this event, anterior to that, posterior to that; the business of dying takes time, even if the expert judges death an event in this or that case 'instantaneous'. Yet in the biography of the one who died, it is most emphatically not an experience, something which he or she can begin to imagine. For what it is for experience to cease absolutely is something which lies beyond the limits of the conceivable. If death is compared as, for instance, by Socrates in the *Phaedo*, to a prolonged dreamless sleep, the comparison breaks down in that from the longest sleep we can imagine we must surely awaken; (if indeed it is in any sense properly called sleep). Is a sleep from which one never wakes sleep? Surely not. It is as if the philosopher is grasping at what seems to him to come nearest the unimaginable, inconceivable state of ceasing to be in any sense an experiencing subject. But between interruption, however indefinitely prolonged, and cessation of consciousness, there is a great gulf fixed, the gulf between the relative and absolute. The transition from the one to the other involves (in the traditional phrase), a metabasis *eis allo genos*. We are engaged with that which transcends our comprehension, and eludes negatively the reach of our conceiving.

Of course we know, in part at least, what we fear in death; for intimations of mortality are with us all the time. We are continually reminded that ahead of us lies the 'bourne from which no traveller returns'. It is not only that those we have known and cared for have taken their leave of us never to return; it is that sometimes gradually, sometimes rapidly, they cease to be missed; their place is filled, and we find ourselves forgetting them. After their death oblivion awaits the life of countless myriads of human beings.

No one has written more profoundly of the presence of death as universal menace, overhanging all that is precious, than William Shakespeare in his Sonnets.

'Then of thy beauty do I question make,
That thou among the wastes of time must go,
Since sweets and beauties do themselves forsake,
And die as fast as they see others grow,

And nothing 'gainst Time's scythe can make defense,
Save breed, to brave him when he takes thee hence.'

So Shakespeare in the pitiless, interrogative realism of his
12th Sonnet. Nothing is spared, all goes down into the dust. We
are as if we had not been; our place quickly filled, our only
immortality in our children; and they too must follow us.

In his 64th Sonnet Shakespeare returns to the same theme.

'That Time will come and take my love away,
This thought is as a death, which cannot choose
But weep to have that which it fears to lose.'

We weep because we have that which we fear to lose. It is as if
the very world of the intrinsically excellent is affected by the
transience which is necessarily part of all that is human.

But is there no hope of immortality? What we have to face is
that any hereafter which we can represent to ourselves in
significantly human terms is inadmissible. For death cuts away
the very context within which alone a genuinely human life is
conceivable. The concept of survival entails that of continuing
memory, and with death the necessary conditions of
remembering, whether actual or dispositional, are destroyed.
Brain and central nervous system are subject to total corruption.
It may be argued that effective recollection, apart from such
conditions, is logically conceivable; but is it causally admissible?
And even if we allow ourselves to entertain the concept of such
activity, what sense can we attach to its exercise under
conditions from which the constants that provide the setting for
that experience are necessarily absent? I mean, for instance, the
conditions under which alone we can lay hold of an objective
time-order to which we can relate, and from which we can
distinguish the flow of our personal experience. For time itself,
so often inevitably mentioned when we seek to realize the threat

of death, or to represent to ourselves that growth in grace for which we may sometimes dare to hope hereafter, is not something that we lay hold of apart from certain cosmological conditions which belong to the setting of our mortal life.

Much that is written on the subject of survival fails to measure up to the principle that death is indeed human kind's 'last enemy'. Too often such writing is little more than easy indulgence of imagination, or rather 'fancy'. We allow ourselves slackly to imagine continuity of experience which neglects not only the pervasiveness of impending mortality, but also the close inter-weaving of characteristically human existence with circumstances that cannot be projected beyond the grave.

Yet Shakespeare, in whose Sonnets we find an unequalled depth of realism concerning the ineluctable condition of our mortality, writes in his 65th Sonnet—

'Or what strong hand can hold his swift foot back,
Or who his spoil of beauty can forbid?
O, none, unless this miracle have might,
That in black ink my love may still shine bright.'

The poet's writing is a memorial of his love that does endure, and by enduring it confers upon that transient, precious experience a kind of immunity from the common fate. If to speak of such achievement as immortal is to use extravagant language, at least it advertises the *monumentum aere perennius* that genius can fashion, establishing its presence as contemporary with successive generations. There is a *mystery* here: I use the word in the sense which the late M. Gabriel Marcel made familiar, to stand for an ultimate which evokes reverence, which elicits a questioning which goes beyond that which receives its answer in the solution of a *problem*.

But what are we to say of the status of this immortality which men and women fashion for themselves by bestowing on their work the impersonal objectivity of the written form, adding as it were to the furniture of the world a means whereby the consciousness of their successors is altered? Certainly this addition to the furniture of the world is a way by which their permanent presence, their continuing efficacy as agents, is secured. Of course, what may be claimed for the poet must also be claimed for men and women of other sorts of genius, for thinkers and for men of action, and for those in whom thought and action are wonderfully one. Yet when we think of those of whom we say that they have not left the world as they found it, we have to recollect the threat of dissolution that hangs over all things human. Where poetry is concerned, we cannot forget that the manuscripts of the majority of the tragedies of Aeschylus and Sophocles were destroyed in the fire that burned to the ground the great library at Alexandria. There is, indeed, a *mystery* here, a veritable point of departure for speculation, an analogue, it may be, whereby to approach the strange reality of survival. Yet the conditions of human existence are not transcended; for the possibility of *pourriture* remains. The monument is more lasting than bronze; yet like bronze it is vulnerable. One may say that such creation is emancipated from the law of coming to be and passing away, which is the law of human, of animal, and indeed of vegetable existence. It is enabled to assume a permanence akin to that of the ancient hills, and by the way it mediates to successive generations the painfully wrought insights of its author, it makes the men and women of later generations his contemporaries. So, indeed, they are the contemporaries of those who, in thought and action, have enlarged the possibility of human existence, of the saints as well as of the men and women of genius, even of Christ himself. Yet dare we call such permanence absolute, or is the immunity from destruction only relative?

Here indeed is the *mystery* which evokes our reverence, the mystery of the insinuation of timelessness into time, of immortality into the world of mortality. But that insinuation is not presented as achieving the defeat of the 'last enemy'. The enemy remains unconquered; that which we cannot visualize or imagine hangs over us all the time, death in which human existence runs into nothingness. If the poets enable us to lay hold on the uniqueness of word written and work wrought, their quality as intimations of mystery, they still leave unbridged the gulf between relative and absolute. No tapestry of metaphor, however marvellously woven, can render intelligible to us the end which awaits us all, or the manner of its overcoming, if, indeed, it is overcome.

If these somewhat disjointed reflections on the gravest of human themes are to include a theological comment, it must surely be that where the theology of death and immortality is concerned, an essentially negative theology must be enabled to have the last word. Authentic theological discipline must take the form of compelling us to understand that what we seek to conceive is inconceivable, is indeed as Wittgenstein insists, not an experience but the term of all experience. If, theologically, we look for a word of hope, we may perhaps find it in the lines of the English Puritan poet Richard Baxter—

> 'Christ leads us through no darker rooms
> Than He went through before;
> He that into God's Kingdom comes
> Must enter by this door.'

PART B

Chapter 7

POWER POLITICS AND RELIGIOUS FAITH

(The Fifth Martin Wight Memorial Lecture)*

In choosing a subject for this lecture, my mind turned to two books: both published during the war years, the first in 1941, Aldous Huxley's *Grey Eminence*[1]: the second at its very end, Arthur Koestler's *The Yogi and the Commissar*.[2] The titles of both have been incorporated into the language. The former was not its author's invention; but his use of it as the title of his study of Father Joseph won it a near universality of currency. So Lindemann is still spoken of as Churchill's scientific *éminence grise*.[3] But the title of Koestler's essay, though less heard today, advertises dramatically a very important bifurcation of approach to the problems of human life and society, the one typified by the devotee in his ashram, the other by the commissar, the dedicated 'social surgeon' serving the cause of the total transformation of a given human society in the light of the directives of the party to which he belongs. But of course there is an important sense in which in Father Joseph, the subject of Huxley's book (which was incidentally a very well researched piece of work), the two life-styles are to a considerable extent conjoined. Father Joseph is at one and the same time the devoted fanatical Capuchin, the father-founder of the Calvarian order of nuns and the skilled, ruthless agent of

* This lecture was delivered at the London School of Economics on Thursday, 8 March 1979.
  [1] London, 1941.
  [2] London, 1945.
  [3] Professor Raymond Page has told me that it is found possibly for the first time in Alexandre Dumas' novel: *Les Trois Mousquetaires*.

Richelieu's purposes. He was no yogi, still less a commissar, but a man whose spiritual teachings rate an admittedly short and critical reference in Bremond's famous history of seventeenth century French spirituality, and one who played an unquestionably important part in the diplomatic history of a period, wherein diplomacy might well be characterized as war carried on by other means.

In the writing and lecturing which Professor Martin Wight devoted to the problems of international politics, we can see the influence over him of his prolonged and deeply critical study of Dr Arnold Toynbee's *A Study of History*. But both in an address which he delivered on 4th February 1951, in Great St Mary's Church in Cambridge and elsewhere he seemed to find a solution for himself of the problems which Toynbee's writings raised concerning the course of human history, in the traditional Christian eschatology. Thus one encounters quite frequent quotations from the so-called 'Little Apocalypse' of the Synoptic Gospels, the discourse which in Mark XIII (and in the significantly different parallel chapters of Matthew and Luke), Jesus is portrayed as delivering at the end of his public ministry. In this discourse warnings relating to 'the end of the world' are interwoven with predictions concerning the destruction awaiting Jerusalem in less than forty years after the date on which the discourse is represented as being delivered. 'Nation shall rise up against nation.' Even reference to the manifestation of anti-Christ was quoted by Professor Wight as suggesting that an extreme pessimism concerning progress towards a possible international order was perfectly compatible with an underlying and enduring hope. 'But then look up; for behold your redemption draws nigh.'

Yet the kind of 'schism in the soul' that is here depicted in terms of what may be called a vision of history, is most certainly also discernible within individuals. The ethical problem of the relation of the saint to the statesman was raised unforgettably by

Plato; but we still wait for anything which deserves to be called a serious step towards its solution. The student of ethics, especially if he is concerned with the relation of ethics to religion (if his study is to relate itself to the concrete, and not escape into a world of easily manageable abstractions) must attend to the way in which in individuals' lives the conflict works itself out. And here the history of the statecraft of Richelieu and his Capuchin 'grey eminence', Father Joseph, has the right to be regarded as of a classical significance. This most especially if one takes into account the man who has considerable claim to be regarded as Richelieu's most powerful opponent amongst the *dévots*, Pierre Cardinal de Bérulle. A professional historian of this period with whom I have discussed the theme of this lecture,[4] even remarked tentatively that had Bérulle lived to be among those who confronted Richelieu and whom he defeated, on the so-called 'Day of Dupes' in 1630, the issue of that encounter so crucial for his personal position, might have gone differently.

It was the famous French student of the New Testament, the Abbé Alfred Loisy, who claimed that 'it was the Kingdom of God which was expected; it was the Catholic Church that happened'. No critical student of the New Testament can escape the question of the relation of the Kingdom of God or the Kingdom of Heaven to the visible Church. There is one strand and one only in the gospel–tradition, in which they seem sometimes to be virtually identified, and that strand is confined to one element in the gospel according to St Matthew.[5] But in the imaginations of the three men we are concerned with in this lecture, the identification is more or less complete. Yet paradoxical as it may seem, in practice it emerges that it is Richelieu for all the concentrated ruthlessness displayed in his

[4] Professor Geoffrey Parker, F.B.A of St Andrews University, to whom this lecture owes a great deal.
[5] It is Matthew who never speaks of the Kingdom of God, always the Kingdom of Heaven (basileia tōn ouranōn).

pursuit of national goals, who alone of the three shows certain reservations where the consequences of this identification are concerned.

Professor Georges Pagès concludes his study of the *Thirty Years War* with the following judgement;[6]

> There can be no doubt that France, and more especially Cardinal Richelieu, were instrumental in helping to accomplish the complete transformation of Europe, this final break with the past which was completed during the last convulsions of the Thirty Years War. We should not think that Richelieu foresaw this or in any way wished it; but he did realize that only a league of Protestant powers maintained and led by his King could prevent the House of Habsburg from establishing its hegemony over Europe. Both he and Father Joseph, his adviser during the struggle, hoped that in this way the balance between the two parties could be maintained, and that Catholicism would at least be able to preserve the position it had kept or recovered. In this he succeeded; it is no less certain that in order to succeed, he accepted a sort of secularization of European politics as well as the division of Europe into distinct Churches and states. By widening the frontiers of the Thirty Years War, French policy, the policy of Richelieu, created the modern Europe which emerged from the Peace of Westphalia.

'Europe became a secular system of independent states.'

The language of this judgement stresses the secular, this-wordly focus of Richelieu's policy in international affairs. His statecraft was not confessional in the sense in which at the time of the crisis of the 'Day of Dupes', Marillac who with the Queen-Mother, Marie de Médicis, under whose protection the Cardinal had earlier survived, may be correctly described as pursuing confessional policies. Whatever their personal motives in seeking to dislodge the Cardinal from his position of unique authority, these opponents took very seriously the fact that he

[6] I quote from the English translation (London, 1970), pp. 250–51.

was resolved to resist a spread of Spanish power, and that for this end, he was prepared to pay the price of lending the support of French military resources to the Protestant side in the Thirty Years War. To acquiesce in the further advance of Habsburg power simply because Philip IV (as Philip II before him) had apparently succeeded in selling himself to the Catholic world as the paladin of the forces of the Counter-Reformation (a dignity which the Pope Urban VIII, was in fact unwilling to concede him) was something to which Richelieu was adamantly opposed. And this opposition, as indeed his policy in the earlier affair of the Valtelline had proved beyond question, was the implementation not simply in theory but also in action of a consciously formulated intention. It was certainly true that on the 'Day of Dupes', Marillac could point to the utterly deplorable state in which so many of the French people lived, as argument in favour of a policy orientated towards domestic reform rather than towards various adventures which could themselves only succeed at the cost of inflicting damage on the great nation that had made the cause of the repression of heresy its own. If successfully pursued, this policy could but help perpetuate the infidelity of other nations and principalities, which whether they stood religiously in the following of Martin Luther or of John Calvin, were agreed in repudiating the authority of the successor of St Peter in Rome, and in following ways of Christian life very far from that newly redefined through the decrees of the Council of Trent. The crisis of the 'Day of Dupes' followed very quickly on the siege of La Rochelle, where Richelieu's 'grey eminence', forsaking the corridors of power which he trod with such uncanny skill, seemed to regain something of his supposedly lost Capuchin innocence in the ardour with which he fulfilled the duties of a military chaplain, tirelessly ministering to the soldiers involved in the siege, offering to them both the consolations of the Catholic religion and the inspiration of his rhetoric. For the man who had complemented the foundation of the Calvarian order of nuns by perpetrating in laboriously contrived Vergilian hexameters, the epic of a future crusade—the *Turciad*—was one who found the rhetoric of holy war unusually congenial. His love of austerity found a ready outlet in the harsh discipline of the camps in which he ministered, and his devotion exultant expression in celebrating the Mass of All Saints Day, 1629, in a Church in La Rochelle restored to the use of Catholic worship.

And here of course the *dévots* were at one with the Cardinal and the Capuchin. It was however a community of purpose which extended no further than the reduction of this great Huguenot community stronghold; a fact that emerges from the details of Richelieu's relations with Bérulle over the affair. The Oratorian whose crucial importance in the development of French spirituality and indeed theology in the period when at last the full impact of the Counter-Reformation began to be felt in that country cannot be denied, advocated a far more uncompromising attitude to the Huguenots than the Cardinal. For to him they were before all else heretics, and the damage they did by their presence was damage to the souls of men.

It is indeed the relative moderation of the Cardinal's treatment of the Huguenots, regarded as a religious minority, that earned him at one time the reputation of being a champion of toleration, almost in spite of himself. In fact he remained constant to the policy of the Edict of Nantes, while rejecting completely the 'Brief' attached to the Edict which secured the Huguenots' right to the use of their strongholds. His early years as Bishop of Luçon showed him ready to use his authority to reshape the life of his diocese in accordance with the decrees of the Council of Trent. He was a prelate of the Counter-Reformation, and it is by no means uncharacteristic of his style that he was careful to seek from the Pope himself dispensation from the priestly obligation of the recitation of the Breviary office daily in its entirety, when the volume of his work as

92

statesman put the proper fulfilment of this religious duty beyond him. His writings included essays in apologetics, and where his own *Apologia pro Vita Sua* was concerned, the evidence of his *Political Testament* and of the writings of the many pamphleteers he enlisted in his service to promote his policies by explaining them, combined to show that it was as a *Catholique d'état* that he presented himself to the world. If he believed and said that the Huguenots could be won back to the Catholic Church by persuasion, it was partly becuase he believed that any attempt to pursue an alternative policy, one of *compelle intrare*, was doomed to provoke as a backlash the recreation of the very state of affairs which he had been determined to end in Béarn and crucially at La Rochelle. He acted to eliminate the peril to the unity of the French state, of a 'state within a state', a fortified enclave disposing of sufficient force to defend itself effectively against attack and by reason of the way of life embodied in and sustained by its institutions, commanding the first loyalty of those who lived within it. The situation was especially dangerous, if such enclaves were so situated geographically that they could be sustained by help from without as in the case of La Rochelle, where the threat of English intervention created a serious problem. Any hope to deflect England from such adventures through the marriage of Charles I (in his last year as Prince of Wales in 1624) to the French king's sister had been disappointed. The influence of his father's beloved Charles Villiers, Duke of Buckingham, over the new king, was far stronger than any corrective that might have been forthcoming from his young wife and her entourage. Thus the establishment of the authority of the state demanded the reduction of La Rochelle; but to follow up the restoration of public worship, according to the rites of the Catholic Church in that city, by a fanatical policy aimed to compel the Huguenots to re-enter the Catholic fold—that way lay disaster.

The total collapse of statecraft which issued in the massacre of

St Bartholomew's Eve, 1572, had made inevitable intensive discussion, among those who might have been its victims, of the right to revolt. Duplessis-Mornay in his *Vindiciae contra Tyrannos*[7] had offered an impressively balanced account of the conditions under which such a right might be exercised, always in his view only under the direction of those properly qualified to initiate it, whom he called magistrates. But others might well have been tempted to use his arguments, invoking (as often he did) for instance the ambivalent attitudes towards kingship in the Old Testament, to draw from them far less restrained conclusions. Certainly a study of this work does much to make intelligible the considerations of expediency which helped to lead to the crisis of Richelieu's relations with the *dévots*.

There is a very great deal here to fascinate anyone seriously concerned with the relations of religion and ethics, even if he must always recall (as I must) that he is not a professional historian and that he is therefore certain to overlook details and nuances of the actions which he is studying, wherein their deepest significance may be found. But to trace even in outline the interplay of Richelieu's religious commitment with his statecraft is to be aware of a paradox. It is out of his remorseless dedication to a power-political purpose that he is constrained to halt the religiously destructive fanaticism of the *dévots*. In his illuminating study—*Constitutionalism Ancient and Modern*—the late Professor C. H. McIlwain drew an important distinction between two elements in government, to which he referred by the terms, *gubernaculum* and *jurisdictio*.[8] Under the former he comprehended all that belonged to decisive action taken in the

---

[7] Professor Parker has warned me that Duplessis-Mornay's authorship of this work (taken more or less for granted by Professor Quentin Skinner in Vol. 2 of his *Foundation of Modern Political Thought*, Cambridge, 1979) should not be regarded as more than extremely likely.

[8] Ithaca, 1940.

name of the state's very existence, while under the latter all that concerned rights whether of individuals or of groups which must be safeguarded, limitations on power that must be acknowledged, etc. A very distinguished Roman historian[9] teaching in Oxford shortly after the last war, lamented that in those years students returning to their books seemed bored by detailed treatment of the device of *senatus consultum ultimum*, (the granting of special emergency powers to the consuls by the Senate for special purpose and limited period during the Republic), but fascinated by all that was involved in the concept of *imperium*, as if their experiences during the terrible preceding years had made them more interested in power and its exercise than in the subtle, often frustrated efforts at its effective civilization. The two moments in government which this historian set over against each other correspond more or less to McIlwain's contrast. Certainly for Richelieu it was the element of *gubernaculum* which mattered; the unity of France must be established on a monarchical basis and according to principles which acknowledged the primacy of foreign over domestic policy. The very concept of that unity was something only properly defined if France were enabled to stand over against Spain as a concentration of power to be reckoned with. We owe to one of Professor McIlwain's pupils, Professor W. F. Church, a very detailed analysis of Richelieu's conception of *raison d'état* and a presentation of the pamphlet literature in which in controversy with such critics as his one-time agent Michel de Mourgues, through his own writings, and still more through the voluminous outpourings which he promoted, he articulated his understanding of the concept of *raison d'état* against the Machiavellians and the heirs of the *Politiques* on the one hand and on the other, against both those who pleaded for Catholic

[9] Professor Arnaldo Momigliano.

confessional policies and those in conscience, compelled to resist them.[10]

In 1595, in his work *De la Sagesse*, Pierre Charron (giving as Professor Church has said, a more autocratic flavour to the concept of royal sovereignty than Bodin) had written:

> The state, that is to say the exercise of power and authority, or rather the clearly defined order in matters of command and obedience, is the support, the cement and the soul of human things; it is the very bond of human society which otherwise could not subsist; it is the vital spirit which in fact makes it possible for so many multitudes of men and indeed the whole nature of things to draw their breath.[11]

The language seems extravagant, the metaphors even nearing contradiction, e.g. 'bond', 'cement', 'soul', etc. But in a single long sentence Charron goes some way to capturing the essence of the need that Richelieu served, including in his service concern that the monarch who was its constitutive foundation, should by his personal appearance, the clothes he wore, the furnishings of his palace, convey visible signs of its dignity and its strength. The rules to be followed by monarchs in their ruling and by those who served their government, were not those which a man should observe in his personal life. The king, as king, was not only permitted, but obliged to act in ways that ignored the dictates of traditional morality. Richelieu was often at pains to make sure that this very special obligation was fully understood by the king's confessor. Yet because so to act was a matter of obligation, the monarch as an individual human being was very far from set free to live as he liked. The same discipline which forbade the destructive fanaticism of a confessional policy leading ultimately to subservience to the Spain of Philip

[10] I find it hard to exaggerate my debt to Professor Church's very important book *Richelieu and Raison D'État* (Princeton, 1972), and to his other writings dealing with the history and development of French absolutism.

[11] This somewhat cumbrous translation is my own.

96

IV and Olivarès, must be imposed on any inclination to use privilege of position as an opportunity for self-indulgence. If Richelieu is the architect of a monarchical absolutism that we can only find repellent, he is not serving the cause of tyranny. If his monarch is in a sense constitutionally *legibus solutus*, this emancipation is not a privilege to be exploited in indulgence of any and every caprice. So the king's minister must watch suggestions coming from mistress or favourite as carefully as direction coming from the king's confessor *sub sigillo*.

But what of the rôle of Richelieu's faith? How did he understand the relation of Church and State? He was not a Gallican; yet the detailed history of the Santarelli affair reveals his deep rejection of the Jesuit thesis of Papal supremacy over those who bore secular rule. It should, of course, never be forgotten that he worked at a time in which confessional and political issues were disastrously intertwined, when the Catholic Church in its struggle to reimpose its authority in areas it had lost to Lutheran and Calvinist reformers, was horrendously active as a political force. It could indeed be argued that this involvement of the Church as an institution on one side or another in any and every sort of conflict concerning, e.g. national frontiers, destroyed the possibility of its exercising any kind of remotely effective influence over the way in which international relations were conducted. And this in spite of the remarkable writing on questions relating to the morality of warfare, etc. of such moral and political theorists as the Spanish Dominican theologian, Francisco da Vitoria. The extent to which the Church found itself beholden to Spanish power was crucial; but it was by no means the only factor. It was a nineteenth century Anglican religious, Father R. M. Benson, SSJE,[12] who was the advocate of an austerity of life that very

---

[12] The founder of the Society of St John the Evangelist, the so-called 'Cowley Fathers'.

many today find it hard not to regard as absurd as well as distorted, who also remarked that the so-called 'conversion' of Constantine was the greatest single disaster which the Christian Church ever sustained. Whatever one's reaction to that judgement, it is hard not to find it receiving a measure of confirmation in the frightening interweaving of religious and political in the period of the wars of religion of the sixteenth century and the Thirty Years War. Yet it could be argued that Richelieu animated by a conception of the vital interests of France and serving a vision of the state in which considerations of built-in constitutional safeguards against the abuse of power at the expense of individuals, minorities, etc., were ruthlessly postponed to securing that state's authority, did in fact impose limitations on the sort of internecine conflict born inevitably of religious fanaticism. To him the *dévots* both seemed and were politically blind.

Here study of his relations with Pierre de Bérulle are very significant. Since Aldous Huxley published in 1941 his study of Father Joseph (drawing as it did on the very well documented, but unfortunately unfinished biography of Canon Dedouvres) the Capuchin has lodged himself in the general imagination as the very type of the man whose spirituality has enabled him to banish from his mind any moral scruple which might make the average sensual man hesitate before underwriting and promoting policies calculated to postpone possible settlement of the war that was tearing Europe apart. (The actual history of the secret peace negotiations between Richelieu and Olivarès' agents is admittedly a great deal more complicated than Huxley allows).[13]

But here I would rather refer to the oratorian Pierre de Bèrulle. The detailed information concerning his career to be

[13] See Auguste Leman *Richelieu et Olivarès*, (*leurs négociations secrètes de 1636 a 1642 pour le rétablissement de la paix*) (Lille, 1939).

extracted from de Houssaye's very long, admittedly, hagiographical biography reveals a man of unquestioned spiritual and theological discernment. The Polish historian of political and social ideas, Dr Leszek Kolakowski, devotes a most interesting chapter to his work in his long study of *Chrétiens sans Église*,[14] suggesting that in his spiritual doctrine and through his influence both in the Oratory and over the Carmelite nuns under his direction, the profoundly theocentric forms of mystical religion (with their inspiration in the pseudo-Dionysius) became subject to a Christocentric formation, in other words were made to enter the framework of existing religious dogma and institutions, and were effectively enlisted in service of the Counter-Reformation in France. If Bérulle stood over against the Jesuits on the one hand and Port Royal on the other (for all his influence on St Cyran), he was in his ecclesiology ultramontane, in the Santarelli affair, for instance, very much the Pope's man.[15]

Yet he had been in his early years subject to humanist influences,[16] and there is no gainsaying the clarity, even the depth of his theological perceptions. He shared in and contributed to the seventeenth century revival of interest in Augustine and his presentation of the theology of redemption is in parts profound as well as attractive. Yet the portrait which emerges from de Houssaye's long work is of one who sought to assure the cause of his Church by the ways of intrigue as well as, e.g. by that of the foundation of Carmels. He played his part in advancing Richelieu's policy over the English marriage accompanying Henrietta Maria to England; but it was the

---

[14] NRF: Éditions Gallimard.

[15] At this point I must acknowledge gratefully my debt to Professor Anthony Levi of St Andrews University.

[16] Professor Bernard Williams in his book on Descartes (London, 1978) remarks that it was Bérulle who made Descartes promise to devote himself to philosophy.

restoration of Catholicism in that country which concerned him, in the first instance the relief of the Catholic minority there.

One is made aware of a man who haunted the society of the powerful: one who was certainly not a statesman, not even a man of affairs, but who at bottom had all Joseph's ruthlessness, even if he manifestly lacked the friar's diplomatic ability, even if indeed he was by circumstance as well as by reason of his gifts compelled to move in a different ambience and to seek seemingly different objectives. Further for him the Catholic Church was always identical with the Kingdom of God. This Church Bérulle laboured to re-establish in France with its theology in a measure set free from bondage to scholasticism, its *pietas* a theologically disciplined mysticism, its authority indistinguishable from that of God himself.

Joseph on the other hand is always the author of the *Turciad*, his gaze set on the vision of the last crusade which would go on as it were from the place whereat (under Philip II's influence) it had as it were turned aside after the battle of Lepanto. He was capable continually of resuming the role of Capuchin friar, the tireless, fiercely bigoted preacher of missions, the evangelist whose astonishing feats of evangelistic endurance Dedouvres chronicles in his two volumes in exhausting detail. Yet he was also a very able diplomat, the Cardinal's indispensable agent. If at first he responded to the issue of the battle of the White Mountain as a *dévot*, later his sense that it was only through assertion of French power at the expense of that of Spain that the cause of the crusade for which he had so obsessively pleaded could be brought within reach of attainment, set his mind free to serve Richelieu to the full extent of his remarkable powers.

Huxley in his still fascinating book traces the friar's seeming indifference to the suffering he helped to continue to the emphasis of his spiritual doctrine on the detail of Christ's Passion, reflected in the very name of the order of Calvarian nuns which he so largely brought into being. That there was a masochistic streak in Joseph is undeniable; but more weight must surely be given in understanding him to his eagerness for crusade. He was in his element at La Rochelle when the schisms in his world seemed to come together; but his fanaticism was animated by the relatively remote near-global purpose he sought to advance, namely the advent of the day when Christendom in arms would march together to wrest the Holy Places from the infidel.

Whereas for Richelieu the state had a certain autonomy and he sought as *Catholique d'Etat* to thread an uneasy path between acceptance of the Church's faith and understanding of itself, and his sometimes near rationalist, sometimes almost mystical concern for the assertion of the state's authority, for Joseph it was a vision of the liberating armies of Christendom that haunted his imagination and seemed to dominate his activity. It was for the freeing of the Holy Places from the Turk that he urged ever more ferociously demanding exercises of prayer and penance of his Calvarians. If Professor Pagès is right in associating his name with that of his master in accepting a sort of 'secularization of European politics', we must reckon with the paradox that Joseph did what he did in service of the hoped for renewal of a medieval vision, even no doubt casting himself in imagination for the enthralling rôle of the Bernard or Peter the Hermit of this last crusade.

So the three men stand over against each other; all of them in different ways coming to terms with the realities of power, all of them significant in the history of French spirituality in the seventeenth century, Bérulle indeed a major figure in Bremond's famous history of religious sentiment in France in that century, Joseph only rating a short and very critical entry, minor both in lasting influence, and in the content of his doctrine. All of them in different ways recognized the significance of power in human life. Richelieu emerges in particular as a man lacking in scruple, ruthless, subtle, masterly; (his understanding of the 'power of the press', to speak somewhat anachronistically, one must judge very impressive) ceaselessly battling against ill-health as well as against his enemies within and without France, an alarming and frequently repellent figure. Yet there is a kind of objectivity in his ruthlessness, displayed for instance in the campaign he waged against duelling (moved here no doubt by the memory of the wasteful death of his brother), whose quality of relentless impersonality is impressively displayed in his behaviour over the Bouteville-Chapelles affair. In his Testament he wrote:

> I admit that my spirit was never more moved than on this occasion, when I very nearly assented to the universal campaign. The tears of de Bouteville's wife had touched me greatly; but the streams of blood which had been shed by your nobility which could only be dammed by the shedding of de Bouteville's and Chapelles', gave me the strength to resist myself, and to strengthen your Majesty's resolve to have this man executed, *pour l'utilité de son état*—a course of action which ran as it were dead against the judgement of mankind at large, and *contre nos sentiments particuliers*.

The passage is illuminating. The execution is justified on grounds of its usefulness in deterring others by clear indication that the imposition of the death penalty for the wantonly destructive activity of duelling was seriously intended. But in this individual case for all his memory of his brother's needless death, the enforcement cut across Richelieu's personal affections. Yet the statesman must cultivate at personal cost, his own peculiar style of impersonality. For he is a man who *must* act, whose actions are prescribed by his purposes. Yet those purposes in turn are themselves prescribed in part by the situation with which he has to deal. If we allow an element of genuine creativity to historical individuals (and the Russian

Marxist Plekhanov in his essay on the rôle of the individual in history shows himself aware that there are forms of historical determinism which attention to the achievement and effect of individuals render hardly credible), it is hard to deny such creativity to the Cardinal. If, moreover, we set him over against Bérulle on the one hand and Joseph on the other, we see in him a man who unquestionably raises for us by his actions a whole number of central questions in respect of the relation of religious faith and power politics.

There is first of all, of course, the question of the moral validity of his objectives, namely the achievement of the unity of the French state and its establishment in a position of unchallengeable strength. How far is such an objective one that Christians can endorse? Certainly in such cases the question of the validity of the objective sought is as important as the closely related problem of the means; this though one must never forget that the supposed validity of objectives is in fact partly called in question by the means that have to be taken in order to secure them. It is well known that Professor Martin Wight, whose work this lecture is intended to commemorate, was in his early years moved to embrace a thorough-going Christian pacifism.[17] His pacifism was partly born of disillusion, disillusion which in terms of a realistic analysis of the international relations of the inter-war years, was made inevitable by failure on the part of this country, either to maintain an effective 'balance of power' in Europe, or to grasp the nettle of making the League system work. Professor Wight saw that the latter demanded a readiness to pay a considerable price in terms of limitation of national sovereignty and of willingness to develop power resources adequate to enforce such an international order. He came to see that the new style of statecraft required to achieve such an end was simply not there.

[17] See his article in the periodical (then a monthly) *Theology* for 1936.

And indeed even before the international scene began quickly to darken after Hitler's advent to power in 1933, it was clear that the sub-structure required to allow such statecraft the faintest possibility of success was simply lacking in the post-war world. It may be thought that in his autobiography '*A Great Experiment*'[18] Lord Cecil of Chelwood offered a blueprint of the kind of initiative required to implement such a vision. A careful study of this book can only confirm the judgement that the conditions required to make that vision a reality *were* altogether lacking. But even if they had been there, the statecraft called into play would have had to reckon with power-realities, in other words to play the classical game in a new situation.

Pacifism calls into question not only the ends which on this or that occasion statecraft may promote, but the game itself. For to rephrase Clausewitz' often quoted dictum: 'War itself is but the game carried on by other means'. If the pacifist's inspiration is often Christian, it is an inspiration which at the same time implicitly involves a radical critique of historical Christianity, a critique which in my judgement is almost entirely valid and which must prove radical to a degree hardly envisaged by many of those regarded today as belonging to the theological *avant-garde*. Most fundamentally it sets a question-mark against the attitude of those Christians who are animated by such a vision as that of Father Joseph, namely that of the attempt by force somehow to 'make the world safe for Christianity', or indeed against that of Bérulle, where a profundity of theological perception blurs the searching quality of Christ's rebuke to the 'sons of thunder' who would have called down fire from heaven on a village that had failed to receive their preaching. 'You know not of what spirit you are.'

The impersonality of the true statesman makes his ruthlessness less frightening; further the character of his

[18] London, 1940.

objectives may be so defined as to leave room for admission of the mysterious authority of the 'kingdom not from hence'. Even if those objectives are formulated in terms of the morally ambiguous conception of vital interests, they are patient of criticism; they are not invested with the near-metaphysical invulnerability which inevitably follows from the characterization of an enterprise as a crusade or the identification of its outcome with the future of the Kingdom of God itself.

To speak in these terms is not to suggest for one moment that there is not a crucially important rôle for the Christian in criticism both of political objectives and of the means by which they are pursued; rather it is to imply the reverse. Still less it is to deny the very large measure of validity to be attached to rejection of the so-called Constantinian revolution. In my opinion Burckhardt's judgement on that emperor's character and the motivation of his so-called 'conversion' remains unaffected by the powerful argument of the late Professor Norman H. Baynes' learned Raleigh Lecture of 1929, which has recently been republished.[19] The naked blasphemy of Constantine's slogan *'in hoc signo vinces'* remains an outrage as disastrous in consequence as it is spiritually repulsive in underlying inspiration. But it is rather to insist that if the resources of spiritual insight, supposedly embodied in Christian religious tradition, critically assessed as they must be, are to be made available to check, or rather positively to humanize the practice of international relations, this can only be in recognition that the process in question must be dialectical in character; dialectical in the sense of the early Socratic dialogues of Plato, or indeed in that of the confrontation of Creon and Antigone, an argument whose outcome was profoundly tragic.

[19] *Constantine the Great and the Christian Church*, second edition with preface by Henry Chadwick (Oxford for the British Academy, 1972).

In the lecture which the late Professor Hedley Bull delivered in this series in 1976 on Professor Martin Wight's classification of different approaches to the study of international politics, he contrasted (I hope I do not misrepresent him) the relative qualified optimism that Professor Wight had found in Kant's *opusculum*—*Thoughts on Perpetual Peace*—with the more sombre attitude, reflected in Martin Wight's tendency to quote from the 'Little Apocalypse' of the Synoptic Gospels, mentioned at the outset of this lecture. Kant's remarkable short treatise cannot be discussed properly without reference to the preoccupation with questions of teleology continually manifested in the writings of his last years. Such a discussion would inevitably involve exploration of the clash between a teleological and an eschatological perspective. And Kant as his late short essays on the 'last things' and on theodicy clearly show, was by no means insensitive to the claims of the latter. In fact it could be plausibly argued that it was more consonant with his metaphysical agnosticism, and his insistence on the 'primacy of the practical reason' that he should prefer to speak of an *eschaton* beyond the possibility of imaginable realization than of a *telos* somehow advanced by the gradual prevalence of immanent rationality in the world of human affairs. Certainly his late essay in criticism of all forms of theodicy (including especially the Leibnizian, which in his earlier years he had accepted) shows a total breach with any and every sort of argument directed to present this world as the 'best of all possible worlds', where evils whether physical (*Übel*) or moral (*Böse*) can be justified as constitutive conditions of a not-otherwise achievable good.

In the last act of his play—*Soldaten*[20]—Rolf Hochhuth presents an imagined encounter between Winston Churchill and George Bell, Bishop of Chichester (1929–58) over the

[20] *Soldaten*, Rowohlt Verlag, Reimbek bei Hamburg, 1967.

moral issues raised by the strategic bombing of Germany during the second world war. It was, I repeat, an imagined encounter; yet arguably Hochhuth revealed more about Bell in this scene than Dean R. C. D. Jasper in the pages of his laborious biography.[21] It was very unfortunate indeed that Hochhuth occluded the deep significance of what he was presenting by committing himself to David Irvine's totally unplausible thesis of Churchill's connivance in an alleged conspiracy to contrive the air crash in which the Polish leader, General Sikorski, perished, in order to prevent the latter's constraining the International Red Cross to investigate the Katyn murders. The importance in 1943 of avoiding bitter controversy with the USSR, still bearing the brunt of the land-fighting in the European War, and at Stalingrad, and then in the following summer at the battle of Kursk inflicting vast damage on the Wehrmacht, was a paramount consideration.[22] For this reason Polish pleas for a proper scrutiny of the circumstances of a terrible outrage against their nation had to be over-ridden. And Churchill in spite of his broadcast on 22 June 1941, and all that followed, remained the individual (as the materials assembled in Martin Gilbert's biography and in the second volume of Professor Richard Ullman's study of British involvement in the Russian Civil War abundantly testify), who had been most passionately committed of all statesmen in the period 1918–21, to a policy of maximum support for the forces of Kolchak, Denikin and Kornilov. Indeed this support went to the extent of authorizing the use of gas by British troops co-operating with the 'White Russian' forces, and that not simply by way of reprisal. Now there could be no 'Second Front' in the west till 1944, apart from the Sicilian and Italian landings. So Churchill had to walk delicately. Yet he felt the anger and grief of the

[21] Oxford, 1967.
[22] Especially as there could be no frontal assault across the English Channel that year.

Poles. But their cause *must* be sacrificed. It is a great pity that Hochhuth identifies this sacrifice with acquiescence in Lindemann's alleged contrivance of Sikorski's murder. His substantial point concerning Churchill's predicament could certainly have been made without it.

Churchill is a statesman of Richelieu's style: he does not belong to the worlds either of Joseph or of Bérulle. In his interview with Bell, as a statesman, bearing a statesman's burdens, constrained by circumstance to incur a statesman's guilt, he turns to Bell for pastoral help. He is caught in a situation in which he is forced to ride rough-shod over his feelings for the Poles, to disregard scruples, to refuse to risk the suspected truth of a monstrous action being revealed through impartial investigation. And Bell, whose steadfast courage in loyalty to his moral vision can no more be denied than his concern going back as far as the Nazi *Machtübernahme* of early 1933 for those who stood against Hitler, is blinded by the obsessive character of his pre-occupation with the 'problem of the means' to the reality of the plea directed towards him by the man addressing him, and he fails Churchill at the deepest level. Between prophet-prelate and statesman there is a great gulf fixed. It is the argument of Creon and Antigone over again: a far greater than Creon cast to defend the claims of more than his *polis* in a period of continuing mortal danger against the champion of the authority of other, but equally binding *agraphoi nomoi*. There is a great gulf fixed between the two men; but its revelation as such is only possible after the dispersal of the illusions born of flirtation with any sort of imagined unifying synthesis whether after the styles of Joseph or Bérulle, or indeed of a facile humanist optimism. It may perhaps be seen with the greatest and most enduring clarity only in an eschatological perspective. Certainly such questioning would seem likely to be part of our human lot for a very considerable time to come. It may well be that the deepest relevance of religious faith to the world of international relations (from which we cannot expect the power-political element to be exorcised) will be to ensure that it must never cease to be raised. Yet we have all of us to reckon with the fact that for all our boasted openness of mind, we are likely to continue to prefer the quick, seemingly satisfying answers of the *simplificateur*, whether theoretical or practical or both, rather than acknowledge the tragic stuff of which human existence, in its simultaneous *grandeur et misère*, is fashioned.

Chapter 8

CREON AND ANTIGONE—BOUTWOOD
LECTURES 1981
I

In choosing a subject for the Boutwood Lectures in 1981, it seemed fitting to select a topic which raises in the most acute way the question of the relation of the individual to the state. It may be thought, indeed, by some of the participants in the recently renewed argument concerning the ethical problems raised by the use of nuclear weapons that there is nothing new to be said. At least it would, however, be conceded that the style and the mood of the present protagonists of unilateral nuclear disarmament differs considerably from the style and mood that marked their predecessors of an earlier generation. There is a sensitivity to the political dimension, and in such pamphlets as Sir Martin Ryle's *Towards the Nuclear Holocaust*,[1] a gravity and force of argument fitting in a Nobel prize winner, who is also Astronomer Royal. I mention this pamphlet now; I shall be returning to it later. Yet I should like anyone concerned with the argument of these lectures to admit its importance. The growing mood of revolt against the continuing multiplication of nuclear weapons systems is very far indeed from irresponsible adolescent protest. Of course, such elements can be traced within it; but the charge of irresponsibility is not one that can, or should be, lightly brought against many of those who have identified themselves with this cause.

It is, as I said at the outset, with the relations of individual and state that we are concerned in this matter. I suspect that the most

[1] The Menard Press, 1981.

serious charge brought against those who advocate the unilateralist case, is that of wishing to conjure out of existence the whole world of statecraft, of raison d'état etc. They are judged guilty of a kind of utopianism of the spirit, of flight from the harsh realities of human history, to a never-never land of love and tranquillity. By no means all of those who argue against unilateralists in this way can be written off as determinists in the sense in which historical determinism is a recognisable creed. They include men and women who certainly admit the reality of contingency in human history, of decisions consciously taken, whose consequences were in part, but only in part, foreseen.

And here I should like to refer to work of my own, a broadcast given on the old Third Programme in 1954, eight years after I had served on the Commission of the British Council of Churches, which produced in 1946 the report entitled *The Era of Atomic Power*. This broadcast was entitled: 'Reflections on the Hydrogen Bomb', and in it I sought to raise some of the issues with which I am concerned in these lectures, in particular the claim that there is a necessary irresponsibility in challenging from its foundations the assumption that questions of weaponry are the exclusive concern of those who profess and call themselves statesmen, and that their answers are not fittingly challenged by those who do not bear their burden. This broadcast was certainly controversial; yet it was published in the *Listener* in May 1954 as well as being transmitted twice. It was subject to no censorship of any kind whatsoever, and when I re-read it, I realised that I had received totally different treatment from that meted out to Professor Michael Pentz, the Dean of the Faculty of Science in the Open University, who earlier in 1981 had the greatest difficulty in being allowed to broadcast on the realities of a nuclear holocaust. The difference in treatment is something which I am not alone in finding profoundly disturbing.

In the recent popular life of Dr. Robert Oppenheimer,[2] the author well brings out the extent to which the scientists at Los Alamos knew what they were trying to do, and not only knew what they were trying to do, but did it the more effectively by their enjoyment of the extraordinary enterprise to which they were committed. It may seem a loaded use of words to speak of enjoyment here; but no reader of the book to which I refer can fail to be made aware of the tonic excitement that permeated and held together this ill-assorted team of specialists, bringing success to their enterprise in spite of the antagonisms and suspicions that threatened to disrupt its prosecution. It is an ethical commonplace that men and women often do best what they enjoy doing, and this commonplace receives a further measure of confirmation from the admittedly complex record of Los Alamos. Yet when success in the full sense of 6 August 1945 crowned their labours, it was as if in a moment of time the language, the traditional, often embarrassing language of penitence replaced almost by force the idioms of enthusiasm that had come readily to their lips in the exciting months of preparation.

A modern student might say that the whole debate begins at that point. The decision had been taken and implemented in ways whose details must fascinate the student of human relations, as well as of political institutions and their actual working. But when the moment of climactic fulfilment came, then even if we suspect the language as we are only too well justified in doing, we find men speaking of apocalypse. True, such speech is only too often the sort of linguistic indulgence that we offer ourselves as a substitute for action. What it suggests is certainly not anodyne; but it may act as a kind of intellectual librium or valium, tranquillising energy of mind and will into

---

[2] *J. Robert Oppenheimer, Shatterer of Worlds*: Peter Goodchild (BBC Publications, 1980).

acceptance of the inevitable. The term 'inevitable' is not intended here (I risk repeating myself) to suggest anything deterministic. The history of the development of nuclear weapons from 6 August 1945 to continuing debate concerning the Trident system and cruise missiles is a very long and complex story, where many things were done and many happened which might have been otherwise. We are concerned with things that human beings have done and others left undone, both by their action and their inaction, helping to make the world we live in. Yet this world, which is as it is and not otherwise, has become and is becoming that with which we have to deal, partly, indeed largely, because of choices which, if not our own, have none the less been made in our name. If we say that nuclear weapon systems are part of our environment, we must be careful to recall the way in which we are using the term environment. No officer of the Scottish Tourist Board in possession of his senses would launch a campaign designed to promote Peterhead and Fraserburgh as alternative residential areas for the wealthier aged to the surroundings of Eastbourne, Bournemouth and Torquay. The climate and situation which may make Peterhead an appropriate site for a long-term prison, effectively rules out its suitability for those who, in their declining years, crave a mild climate in the winter months. The distinction of category between climate and weapons systems is of fundamental importance.

Yet when one has at last begun to alert one's conceptual sensitivity to such distinctions, the world of politics, and in particular that of international relations, remains. Its sheer complexity provides a ready arsenal of arguments against those who would be condemned as provoking by their morally indulgent simplifications, the very catastrophe whose possibility moves them to eager protest. 'The best is the enemy of the good.' The phrase is a cliché; yet it is often invoked with telling relevance in argument against those who write and speak as if the internal subtle realities of mutual deterrence can be disregarded.

A serious student of these issues, who is not a specialist in the theory of international politics, is sometimes aware of a chasm, not simply of language, but of outlook between those who, by reason of their special expertise, are more or less at home in that world, and the rest of mankind, who find the realities too horrifying, ultimately too inhuman to envisage for more than the passing moment. This statement is an admitted exaggeration; but it is an attempt to formulate the sense of personal defeat which may invade the spirit of a man or woman who is told that the condition of his or her survival, and that of the institutions under which he or she lives, is a willingness to perpetrate horrors of a sort that seem morally prohibited by any system of ethics, whether religious or humanist, which the individual may profess, however little his or her life may accord in detail with its Credo. For even those of us whose lives least accord with what we profess as of good report, are not lacking all the time in sincerity when we dare to call what seems to us evil by its name.

Of course, it is claimed that only by maintaining such a commitment, only by expressing our readiness in the last resort to use such weapons, will we avoid the need to do so. But we have to ask ourselves whether it is psychologically credible to maintain such a profession, knowing all the while that in the last resort it is intended to draw back, at least from launching the final nuclear holocaust.

It has, however, to be remembered that there is a serious tradition of ethical reflection concerning the limits of the permissible in international warfare. Indeed, a part of this venerable tradition was made the subject of a recent series of Lee-Knowle lectures in Cambridge by Professor Geoffrey Best[3]

[3] *Humanity in Warfare*: Professor Geoffrey Best (Weidenfeld & Nicholson, 1981).

in which, among other subjects, he paid a wholly deserved tribute to the remarkable achievement, in practice as well as in theory, of the International Red Cross. But of course pre-occupation, at least in theory, with the 'problem of the means' has gone on across the centuries, and all students of the history of the last two World Wars must inevitably be aware of its presence, its fragmentary but obstinate persistence, its folly and futility, but also its splendour and its tragedy.

In this connection it is worth mentioning here that in June 1942 General Ludwig von Beck, who until the summer of 1938 had been chief of the German General Staff, gave to a group of which he was a member, a lecture[4] on the political, as well as the moral obliquity of *total war*. The lecture contained many references to Clausewitz, which it might have been thought dangerous to make in such a place at such a time. Beck had his own grave measure of responsibility for the support given by the German Army to Hitler in his earlier years, (though he had been revolted by Roehm's murder in 1934 which, in a sense, consolidated the Army's influence over the régime at that time.) But he came to see the light, and by 20 July 1944, he was fully committed to the tyrant's assassination. When the conspiracy failed, Beck died in a way that for all its peculiar horror has, in retrospect, a genuinely tragic magnificence. I mention Beck if only as offering evidence of the authority of such preoccupation in the mind of a man whose whole training would have impressed upon him the worth of obedience for its own sake.

It may be said that Beck was acting in an extreme situation; but if this is admitted, it makes the almost academic coolness, which disciplines the passionately felt argument of his lecture, all the more impressive. Indeed, it is from that part of his courage that we have most to learn in the very different situation in which we find ourselves. If there is much in Beck's

---

[4] Included in Beck's posthumous *Studien*.

situation which justifies our regarding it as one of extremity, it is most important that we should not allow the recognition to justify indulgence in apocalyptic speculation or rhetorical Jeremiads. If we are concerned with a crucially important aspect of our present human situation, we must first of all seek to kindle argument, to provoke discussion and interrogation, it may be in the first instance with ourselves. If such questioning takes us a long way, the metaphysical style of the journey need not alarm us, or make us fear to seem ridiculous in the eyes of those who have mastered, as maybe we have not, the conceptual technicalities involved, e.g. in thought concerning advanced delivery systems and their like. There are very many ways of darkening counsel in discussion of the ethical problems raised by nuclear warfare; but one of the most effective is the facile invocation of the alleged distinction between fact and value. If in what follows we seem to advance into metaphysical territory, it may be that only by such floundering will we avoid the damaging consequences of saying that such and such a question is question of fact, and such and such a question of value. The need to understand what we are about in this respect is all the greater because in the debates which concern us, there are concepts which slither, and are indeed encouraged to slither by those who use the distinction of fact and value, from the factual to the ethical and back again. The very obvious example is provided by the concept of deterrence with which we shall shortly be concerned.

Of course, the technicalities matter enormously; but what is a technicality? We are certainly exploring an area in which effective strategic, and therefore political study involves a readiness to master a good deal of contemporary physical theory. Moreover it is an area in which theoretical advance is itself fuelled by technological demands. Thus expenditure on space exploration receives part of its justification from the way in which satellite development itself opens the door on new styles of weapons delivery system, immune from the sort of sanction which is an accepted premise of much taken for granted on the subject of strike and counter-strike capabilities. We deceive ourselves if we deny that there is an element of the sheerly exciting in these possibilities; we may feel ourselves a little giddy when we read or hear of them; but the giddiness is not all a matter of fear. The human world remains a wonderful place, if it is also a terrifying one. Nothing excuses those who indulge themselves too easily in pointing out with relish the ambivalence of human progress, as if to question its very reality. At first sight I may seem to contradict myself here, in view of what I said earlier on the subject of men's responsibility for what they bring into being, especially for what touches the place where the human world is inextricably woven together with its natural setting. If I am concerned with abuse of the murky distinction between fact and value, it is because through abuse of that alleged distinction we are prevented among other things from seeing the possible relevance to our whole situation of the concept of temptation.

But I turn now to the concept of deterrence, grateful to such writers as Professor Paul Ramsey[5] and Dr R. E. Jones,[6] for the careful work which they have done in its analysis. We are all of us as I said above familiar with the claim that the existence of strategic thermo-nuclear weapons systems at the disposal of the 'great powers' provides a context within which the business of international relations, and especially the settlement of conflicts, may be carried on without passing over into open war. Of course there is gross over-simplification in such a claim; it is a piece of sheer mythology; for there has been conflict of almost every sort in the years that separate us from 1945. It is rather suggested that there has been and is a tacit contractual agreement between the 'great powers' to use their monopoly of

[5] *The Just War* (Scribner's).
[6] *Deterrence* (Routledge & Kegan Paul).

such weapons to prevent a line being crossed, from which there is no return. The extent to which this model in any way represents the detail of what has actually happened in respect, e.g., of Korea, of Suez, of Hungary, of Vietnam, of Czechoslovakia, of Cambodia, is a question on which an expert on international relations must be allowed to be heard. One is almost certainly justified in finding an element of sheer propaganda in this way of presenting the role of thermo-nuclear armament in the actual course of history in the past 40 years. It is as if an effort was being made to construct the precarious, often frightening exchanges of this decade into a framework that one is seeking to sell as the only acceptable context in the later part of the twentieth century for the conduct of international relations. It is admittedly presented as a device; a device which is all the time accepted by a continuing contractual agreement of all those powers who are in varying degree parties to the circumstances from which initially it arose. But the very language which I have used has masked the most frightening element in the whole situation, and that is its built-in instability. There are, of course, other questions arising out of the realities of nuclear technology; and with some of them I shall be concerned in my second lecture. For the time being I want simply to focus on the factor of instability, recognising that it is a matter both of politics and of technology.

We have to reckon, if we would be realist, with the revolt of the lesser powers against the monopolisation of thermo-nuclear weapons systems by the 'great powers'. Of course, such revolts are variously motivated; they may be born of national pride, or they may spring from much more subtly political considerations. Thus it is argued that possession of the Polaris or Trident systems by the United Kingdom gives to Britain a power which it otherwise would not enjoy, of determining the limits of policy debates. Such an argument has long been recognised as one of the primary impulses behind the acquisition of a small nuclear capability by minor powers, who believe that through such acquisition they may indeed influence the manner in which their major partners exercise their deterrent responsibilities. Of course economic stringency has sometimes acted as a restraining factor in this development, especially now that it is increasingly recognised that missile delivery systems represent more costly technological outlay than the weapons themselves. But such restraints only operate as a partial check on monopoly,[7] as a forced, temporary acceptance of the alienation springing inevitably from the confinement of these capabilities to the major powers. Yet though we may have to reckon with ambitions that circumstances will increasingly frustrate, we cannot deny their reality, or indeed disguise from ourselves the fact that they may be partly fulfilled.

Yet what is happening in the meantime to deterrence? The concept of deterrence is not an ethical concept. It is, of course, admitted that the connection between punishment and deterrence is synthetic in that punishment is necessarily retrospective. A man or woman can only be punished for what he or she has done, whether that punishment in our society is financial or custodial in its form; the concept of deterrence is invoked in discussions of penal theory when it is claimed that our penal system must be judged in part by its effectiveness in deterring would-be offenders by confronting them with the consequences following their commission of an intended offence, and its detection. Thus it is said that certainty or likelihood of detection is a more effective deterrent sanction than severity in the penalty imposed. It is also claimed (and this is important) where certain offences, especially motoring offences, are concerned, that if the law is to be made truly effective as an instrument of protection, deterrence requires to be made much more effective by increase both in scale of

[7] There are also other factors at work of which I shall say something in my second lecture.

119

penalty and extension in scope of police investigation, e.g. by random breath tests. So the concept of deterrence has its place in discussion concerning punishment, which is presumably an ethical matter. But we have to recognise that when we speak of deterrence we are speaking of human motivation, of the sorts of consideration which inhibit human action. Yet because the concept plays a significant part in debate concerning punishment, we tend to invest a deterrent system, imaginatively at least, with a certain numinous quality. It is as if, with that which deters us from action, we are confronted with a divinely established order.

Now theologians across the centuries have made sometimes profoundly influential contributions to political theory, interpreting in their own way, Paul's insistence that government is a structure of divine appointment. There is no doubt that the state's authority has frequently been enhanced by appeal to such recognition of its supposed providential rôle. One would, moreover, claim that deterring men and women from violence or fraud is a significant fulfilment of that rôle. But the deterrence in question is thus invested with a kind of moral dignity because it is always, or should be always in accordance with law. It is not a kind of check or restraint exercised through a system that is profoundly unstable, that is certainly expressive of tremendous achievement, but also in itself a source (I use the word for want of a better), of profound degradation.

Certainly Paul in writing as he did had to reckon with Nero! He was able to detach himself from consideration of that emperor's life-style and attend only to the functional significance of government as an institution. Yet according to tradition in the end both Peter and he suffered death at the emperor's hands in the persecution which followed the fire of Rome. The point of conflict may have been religious rather than ethical. In this present we have to acknowledge a likely duty of opposition at points where ethical considerations assume an overtly religious quality, where for instance we are ordered to accept a total disregard of human dignity in the name of alleged collective necessity. It was the late Professor John MacMurray who, in the first volume of his Gifford Lectures,[8] spoke of Kant as the profoundest critic of any sort of totalitarian ethic. He had in mind that moralist's formulation of the categorical imperative as demanding that we treat human nature, whether in the person of ourselves or of others, as an end and not as a means only. One could say that Kant's language expressed a reverence that went beyond the purely ethical, that conveyed rather an authentic human *pietas*. It is hard to escape conviction that arguments defending reliance on nuclear weaponry always end by seeking to justify in the last resort disregard of this imperative in the name certainly not of individual survival, but of over-riding collective purpose, supposedly able to prescribe its own morality.

In one of the sections of the ethical discussion of his *Republic*, which has genuine claim to be regarded as profound, namely his use of the myth of Gyges in Book II, Plato invites the student to consider the situation of the individual who has made himself by accident of discovery immune from the ordinary restraints that inhibit our behaviour one towards another. If we can, as Gyges could, turn ourselves invisible at will, then no doors are closed to our desires; and (more important) we can subsequently justify at the bar of history the methods we used in the promotion of our ends, by our subsequent actions towards our fellows and towards the gods. The passage has a certain *limited* relevance to our present concerns. The limitation is very important, and I would stress it at the outset. For one thing, we are not concerned with an individual, but with organised human societies; further we are concerned with a race for technological mastery that is going on all the time, that has a

[8] *The Self as Agent* (Faber, 1957).

most important rôle in much that we call space research, fascinating though we may find much of the insight which it brings us. It is not a situation in which one man has secured for himself a capability that sets him apart from his fellows. Rather it is one of striving which is at once exultant and desperate; and the two elements, the element of exultation and the element of despairing fear are both alike important. The moment may come when a combination of political factors with temporarily achieved technological superiority of an intelligible kind, will present one of the so-called 'great powers' with an hour that I can only call one of supreme temptation. But is it not an absurd misuse of words to speak of the modern state as being tempted?

And here, of course, we come up against the central question not of the relation of fact and value, but of the relation of personal morality to the power-realities involved always in international relations, and in the present day in forms of overwhelming gravity. It can hardly be denied that sense of the risk involved in the use of nuclear weapons has given to them a very special significance; for it will certainly be the case that the effects of their use will be passed on in space and in time as those of no other weapon. The history of this century is one that contains examples of the gradual abandonment of restraint in war by powers engaged upon its prosecution, even if we also recall the various examples of individual protest that have been made against such loss of any sort of moral inhibition. The end is immanent in the means, and certainly this century has provided us with innumerable examples confirming that ancient insistence. But what of a situation in which there is risk of the utterly unknown in consequence of the adoption of particular means? This question is one so crucial that it will occupy a good deal of our attention in the second lecture; but if before proceeding I may recapitulate, I would say that so far we have been obsessed by a central question that has not been raised explicitly, but rather has been allowed to permeate the whole argument, and that question is the query whether in this present unilateralism is, or is not, a form of political irresponsibility. If it is not a form of political irresponsibility, how can its significance be shown as something very much more than an abdication from personally unacceptable obligations? There are, no doubt, very many lessons to be learnt from past failures in threading an authentically human path between e.g. the facile optimism that will not look on historical realities as what they are,[9] and a pessimism that has moved too readily from a realistic to a nihilistic posture. The many-sidedness of the effort required by the unilateralist to achieve a posture relevant to the world in which we live is a tormenting one; yet we have to ask ourselves as we try to formulate the outline of such a presence by what criteria we distinguish success from failure in the undertaking.

I conclude this lecture by quoting a paragraph from Sir Martin Ryle's pamphlet, embodying the sort of practical suggestion to which we should surely give serious consideration, not because it embodies any sort of final wisdom, but because it provides a point of departure, provided that we start without illusion concerning the distinction of success from failure in so perilous and precarious an undertaking.

'The first step appears to be a non-nuclear Europe—and here the UK has the key role. When the alternative is annihilation, one must take risks—and no one denies there are many. First there must be a complete removal of all US bases (including submarine detection systems, communication centres and other "facilities" for conducting a nuclear war) and the dismantling of our own Polaris and other nuclear weapons. Some will argue that this would leave us open to a Russian strike; but the risk would be no worse than we run at present and, by reducing the threat which the Russians perceive to be directed at them, it could lead to their agreement to cut down "theatre" and

[9] The work of the late Professor Reinhold Niebuhr is of lasting significance here.

123

"tactical" weapons and the progressive removal of nuclear weapons from the rest of Western Europe.'[10]

APPENDIX TO LECTURE I

If Oppenheimer was profoundly disturbed by the realization of what he had helped to bring about, there was also a significant revulsion of feeling about the whole policy of strategic bombing in the United Kingdom after the war. In his excellent book—*Bomber Command*[11]—Mr. Max Hastings records the bitter anger of Air-Marshal Sir Arthur Harris at the refusal of the authorities to grant a campaign medal to those who had served in Bomber Command, and who had survived the terrible ordeal of their war service. It was as if the memory of e.g. the fire-storm that had marked the great raid on Hamburg in 1943, and still more, perhaps, of the horror of the late raid on Dresden in 1945, ruled out the award of a decoration to men who had certainly included in their number the agents of such events, but who by their sustained and dedicated heroism, had unquestionably earned such. The same men and women who no doubt had applauded the Dean of Chichester's action in denying the pulpit of his Cathedral to his diocesan on 'Battle of Britain Sunday' in 1943, because of Bishop Bell's steadfast fidelity in protest against the policy of obliteration bombing, now allowed weight to their own scruples in a way that seems (not least to those who either whole-heartedly, or more tentatively endorsed the Bishop's action), somehow rather cheap.

Far more edifying, and worthy to be recalled along with Bell's costly witness, is the refusal of the Dean of St Albans (the Very Rev Cuthbert Thicknesse) to allow a special, official service of thanksgiving to be held in St Albans Abbey at the end

[10] Op. cit. p30. It will be remembered that Sir Martin's pamphlet was published in 1981.

[11] Jonathan Cape, 1979; Pan Books, 1981.

of the war with Japan in August 1945; because he judged what had been done at Hiroshima and Nagasaki a moral outrage.

II

One of the most remarkable sermons I have ever heard was preached on Sunday 15th May 1955 in King's College Chapel in Aberdeen by the late Professor Herbert Farmer, the Norris-Hulse professor in Cambridge, whom five years later I was to succeed. He preached on the text: 'Shall we call down fire from heaven to consume them?' His subject was not, of course, the one with which these lectures are concerned, but the much more general topic of the ways of God with men, his patience and the obligation laid upon his creatures, in so far as his revelation and their response to it enabled them to discern it, to seek to imitate it in their dealings with their fellows. But what he said is highly relevant to the issues with which we are concerned.

For it is often claimed and indeed most powerfully argued that the alternative to the deliberate continuance of the policy of the over-all deterrent is in fact submission to an 'armed doctrine'. (The phrase is Edmund Burke's.) If (to refer again to the passage from Sir Martin Ryle's essay which I quoted at the end of my last lecture), we pursue the aim of a non-nuclear Europe, we lay ourselves open to the charge of leaving Western Europe at the mercy of the Marxist-Leninist totalitarians of the East. It may be asked: Who are *we* in this sentence? This is a highly relevant question and one that it is not easy to answer. Tentatively I might say those who find themselves moved by the argument of the last lecture, especially by what was said on the instability of the deterrent system. But what of the totalitarians of the East? Presumably here we have in mind Russia and her satellites. Again we move at the level of question and answer; no precise *akribeia* is possible. Yet in the light of recent events in Poland, it can hardly be denied that that system understood as an organized concentration of power is itself subject to continual internal stress. Of course it would be absurd to speak of its beginning to collapse from within, and serious questions must be faced concerning conditions under which these tensions have developed. Yet those who confront us with the threat of totalitarian dictatorship as an overwhelming argument against the plea for European nuclear disarmament speak as if such dictatorship were a 'Platonic Idea', absolutely immune to any sort of change. Yet elementary students of political theory know that Marxism *has* undergone very many changes, and that on the plane of action as well as of theory. The Marxist world is a very complex place, and includes more than, for instance, such abominations as the debasement of psychiatric practice to elicit conformity with the Party's chosen line.

The Leninist development was certainly crucial in this respect; so too was the Stalinist. But the Leninist development, as much as that which followed Stalin's succession, was a development on the plane of practice as much as that of theory, and one which at that level has still to be answered. Arguably it is for such an answer that we are at present groping, and it could be said that if these lectures have any value, that value lies in their attempt to articulate a little of what a valid response in this present might involve.

It will be claimed, however, that in what I am now saying I am blandly ignoring political realities, speaking as if national states, (and the existing international state systems, especially N.A.T.O.), were not part of our world, were not, indeed, among the foci calling for our allegiance. The national state demands our loyalty because through its institutions, in particular by reason of the extent to which it upholds the rule of law, it provides the framework of our everyday existence, and also because through these same institutions it mediates to us our cultural inheritance. Without its protecting power, made effective on the international plane by N.A.T.O., little would remain of our freedom of thought, our right to innovate in the arts, and critically to continue traditions of investigation and discovery in the sciences.

It may be worthwhile here to look at a *part* of Hobbes' very complex argument for absolutism, doing this not as scholars but as those who would learn lessons in political theory from elements in that remarkable apology for unchallengeable state sovereignty. Hobbes invites those of his readers who shrink from the kind of political authority he defends to ponder life without it. Such life would inevitably degenerate into a state of incipient war, with life, poor, solitary, nasty, brutish and short. If we disallow both the sovereign's unchallengeable monopoly of coercive force, and its right to use that force for our protection, we risk being plunged into a terrifying insecurity, in which our uncertainty and fear of what others may be purposing against us, will drive us towards undisciplined violence in our own protection. If by our initiative we undermine the state's capacity to protect us, we are preferring our own little personal scruples and their indulgence, to that security which is the foundation of decent life, both for ourselves and for our fellows.

There is no escaping the problem of power, that problem of which, in different ways, the great political theorists have helped us to become aware, from which Utopians are always tempted to flee. In his autobiography—*A Great Experiment*[12]—the late Viscount Cecil of Chelwood developed an apology for the League of Nations in frankly Hobbesian terms. The League's chance of establishing peace among the nations in the years following the end of the First World War, depended upon its effective monopoly control of the military force which the powers that made up its membership had at their disposal.

[12] Jonathan Cape, 1941.

Hobbes had predicated of his sovereign an unchallengeable monopolisation of the means of coercion; Cecil believed that the League might have succeeded if it had enjoyed an analogous near monopoly of the necessary means of international coercion. It is tempting to suppose that Cecil's model could be applied to the world of the nuclear deterrent, with a kind of supremacy vested in the alleged 'balance of terror'. But it would be a deadly mistake to argue in any such way. Certainly Viscount Cecil was not envisaging a situation in which the system of coercion was created, not as the expression of a common readiness to submit disputes to an effectively superior arbiter, but as the product of a necessarily unstable form of power. We are, in fact, in a situation in which weapons systems do not serve the institutions which claim to control them, but rather by their internal dynamism quite largely determine the way in which the institutions in question operate.

Consider the phrase: monopolisation of the means of coercion. That phrase suggests that we are dealing with instruments that we can effectively control, submitting their use, at least in principle, to rules that we can establish and indeed go on to interpret in ways which can claim to be quasi-legal, even if there is no judicial authority concerned to distinguish valid from invalid interpretation. Of course some methods of coercion lend themselves more easily to control than others, and there are those which give rise to very special problems, for instance the use of nerve gas and plastic bullets in riot control. Whatever may be said against a continuing presence of the British armed forces in Northern Ireland, it is hard for anyone to deny that the situation there would be improved if arms of every sort used in the violence there, were wholly concentrated in the hands of the security forces, and not made available, it may be on grounds of ill-considered sentiment, to para-military practitioners of merciless sectarian violence. Such monopolisation may be practically a task of the greatest difficulty, even as it would not be likely to do more than secure a breathing space for human decency to begin to prevail as a determinant of conduct over present religious and national frenzies. Yet for all its elusiveness of attainment and likely limitation in positive consequence, a temporary alleviation through termination of the irresponsible traffic in arms is at least conceivable, and not entirely despicable as an objective, especially if one considers the daily toll of victims totally innocent of religious or political offence, and the mounting tide of bitterness between the opposed communities, which increasing violence can only help to raise to even more appalling heights.

The inheritance of history weighs heavily against even this possibility. But the scenario is a credible one, because (to repeat) the deadly instruments involved are manageable in a way in which continually changing forms of nuclear armament are not likely to be.

On page 16 of his pamphlet, Professor Ryle quoted the remarkable words of the late President Eisenhower in his farewell address:

'This conjunction of an immense military establishment and a large arms industry is new in military experience. . . . We must guard against the acquisition of unwarranted influence . . . by the military-industrial complex. The potential for the disastrous rise of misplaced power exists and will persist.'

It will be remembered that these words provide a kind of text for the remarkable book written shortly after they were spoken, by the American sociologist, the late Professor C. Wright Mills—*The Power Élite*. It would be valuable to have a new edition of this book, which would include explicit treatment of the role of the nuclear industry in promoting e.g. in the Pentagon, the claims of each successive innovation in hardware which the technological expertise at its command has suggested and begun to develop. It is a great mistake in analysing statements concerning monopolisation and control of nuclear armament to neglect the interests of vast concentrations of industrial power and resource in promotion and development of such instruments of destruction. No one could accuse Eisenhower of sentimental pacifism; but it is perhaps equally hard, whatever the shortcomings of his presidency, to deny his claim to have spoken a prophetic word at his leave-taking.

It may be said that the sort of argument which I have advanced here leads to a kind of Luddism. Certainly, to advocate not as a solution, but as an approach to fundamental problems of political existence, rejection of the sorts of advance in so-called defensive technology that the development of the exact and applied sciences has made possible, lays me open to just such a charge. Yet the quotation of Eisenhower's words should remind the student that the sorts of changes under consideration have not taken place in a kind of economic and cultural vacuum, unaffected by a whole number of pressures, many of them most certainly undeserving of acceptance as forms of disinterested patriotic concern. What I would plead for is that we recognise the sheer magnitude of the changes that have been allowed to take place, that have, indeed, been imposed willy-nilly upon us. When we acknowledge their scale, we may begin to see the need for what I might dare to call a Copernican revolution of mind and spirit, in particular of imagination. For, of course, these changes are, in the forms in which we have received them, a perverted practical expression of the radically transformed understanding of the world in which we live, of the universe of which we are part, which belong to our contemporary inheritance. The Marxist-Leninist is right to stress the unity of theory and practice, and if we are his critics, we must learn from him the extent to which the very sense of fundamental theoretical change may be distorted, indeed profoundly perverted by a corrupt politics.

Here I return to Professor Farmer's sermon, to which I

referred at the beginning of this Lecture. 'Shall we call down fire from heaven to consume them?' When one is aware that cosmological advances have transformed our image of the world, and yet from mathematical incapacity is unable to make one's own the changes that have taken place, one ought in humility at least to acknowledge that one's intellectual poverty impairs one's response to the new whole of which one is part. This is badly put: but what I want to suggest is that we ask ourselves whether or not incapacity to make our own the great theoretical changes in *Weltanschauung* of the last decades is not vitiating our sense of the way in which on the whole advances are being realised humanly in perverted form. Because intellectually we remain obstinately pre-Copernican, we are too easy prey to those who sell us, or seek to sell us the claims of a perverted technology, including those who are more motivated by considerations of company or personal profit than by concern for human rights and threatened personal freedoms. If we make ourselves the prey of the forces I mention, we indeed join our voices to those who would call down fire from heaven, and consume our foes. Thereby we not only destroy those who threaten us, but ourselves menace the whole human future, making it harder (if not altogether impossible), for those who come after to measure up to the heights of their obligations.

But power realities remain, and it would be totally absurd to pretend that we can escape by a new style of spirituality, the intractable and the tragic.

The conflict of Creon and Antigone is still with us. In my first lecture I criticized the apocalyptic mood: there is, of course, in a proper patience (of the sort for which Professor Farmer pleaded), an authentic remedy for apocalyptic indulgence. Such a patience, profoundly disciplined in its every expression, was realised archetypally by the One to whom the "sons of thunder" put their question. Yet we have to ask ourselves again whether we have the right to advocate courses of action which must involve the possibility, even the likelihood of incalculable waste in their outcome. We must always shun apocalyptic indulgence and the cult of despair, scrutinizing all the time, strenuously enlarging the reach of our rationality. We must, of course, be affected by what, in the first lecture, I called metaphysical considerations; we must be moved by thought of what we *believe* ultimately to be the case. I say *believe*; for here we speak of that which we cannot know, and which is a matter of faith.

When John Milton wrote his sequel to *Paradise Lost*, his 'brief epic' *Paradise Regained*, he confined himself more or less to a detailed study of Christ's temptation in the desert. His treatment was no doubt influenced by contemporary and recent exegesis from the worlds of Renaissance and Reformation alike. Further, modern students of Milton's life and work have emphasized the extent to which, together with *Samson Agonistes*, it bears witness to his deep political disappointment, following the restoration of Charles II in 1660; (the poems were published in 1671).[13] It will, of course, be pointed out by others that where his Christology was concerned, Milton was an Arian; yet such consideration in no way detracts from the profundity of his achievement any more than the validity of his understanding of the cost of patience is queried by recollection of the school of personal, political disappointment in which he learnt its sense.

I offer an extended quotation from the fourth book (Lines 541 to 561)

'So saying he caught him up, and without wing
Of Hippogrif bore through the Air sublime

---

[13] I owe a great deal to Professor Barbara Lewalski's book *Milton's Brief Epic*. Dr. Christopher Hill argues strongly that *Paradise Regained* and *Samson Agonistes* belong to Milton's later period.

Over the Wilderness and o'er the Plain;
Till underneath them fair Jerusalem,
The holy City, lifted high her Towers
And higher yet the glorious Temple reared
Her pile, far off appearing like a Mount
Of Alabaster, topped with Golden Spires:
There on the highest Pinnacle he set
The Son of God, and added thus in scorn:
   "There stand, if thou wilt stand; to stand upright
Will ask thee skill. I to thy Father's house
Have brought thee, and highest plac't, highest is best.
Now show they Progeny: if not to stand,
Cast thyself down; safely if Son of God:
For it is written, 'He will give command
Concerning thee to his Angels, in thir hands
They shall uplift thee, lest at any time
Thou chance to dash thy foot against a stone' ".
To whom then Jesus: "Also it is written,
'Tempt not the Lord thy God'." He said and stood.'

It is not for nothing that critical students of the poem have found the last four words at once the most elusive and the most crucially important.

Milton deliberately finds the climax of Christ's desert ordeal in Satan's challenge to him to cast himself from the pinnacle of the temple, to put the question of his status to the test, to yield to a fundamental impatience, the end either total victory or nothingness. The words could, I suppose be used to indicate the outcome of a nuclear war; only there the total victory would itself be suffused with the quality of nothingness. The language is vulgar and indulgent, and yet it may be partly justified by those who claim that we must in the last resort be ready to use these weapons, even if we impose on ourselves as well as on our opponents consequences that most certainly cannot be foreseen, but which *might* include something that we could call, if not a total, at least a decisive victory. We deceive ourselves if we deny that in the last resort our fabric of deterrence is partly woven of our resolution to do just this. But we have to ask ourselves whether human beings have any right to take such risks with the world of which they are part. There is, of course, the further question whether any cause justifies the calling down of such fire from heaven.

I make the reference to Milton's epic quite deliberately, thus taking up the reference in my first lecture to temptation. Oppenheimer found himself employing the category of sin, even if he might have said that he was quite ignorant of its theological import. But he spoke as one who by his gifts and public obligations had been thrust into the role of architect of an enterprise whose accomplishment pulled him up short. In a way in which many of us do not, he knew the world which by his action he had helped to make, and to make in a horribly perverted form. His subsequent life is in many ways a sad story, its sadness springing in part from what he had allowed himself to help bring about. Milton saw Christ tempted impatiently to escape the burden of his human existence. We live in an age in which such a temptation is not far from every one of us; for we have to learn anew what it is to be human.

Certainly the bias of my argument is in a unilateralist direction, and it is on that side that I would take my stand. But when I have said that, immediately I must insist to myself that there is no escape from the tragic dimension, illustrated classically in the conflict between Creon and Antigone. Sophocles certainly portrays the woman as the nobler; but the statesman's responsibilities are real, and if we suppose them over-ridden, we must acknowledge that they are genuine, and that the cost of over-riding them may in the immediate future require to be paid. There is no escape from risk, and risk must always be taken not in a mood of self-indulgence, but in one of disciplined self-knowledge. There is call here for the exercise of a rationality that is aware at once of its authority and of its limitations.

PART C

Chapter 9

THE MYTH OF GOD INCARNATE[1]

INTRODUCTORY NOTE

This rather rough comment on the symposium—The *Myth of God Incarnate*—(1977), originally written for broadcasting, is included as an introduction to the christological papers in this volume in as much as it sketches the aspects in which traditional doctrine must be defended, and those others in which by its refusal to face the issues of kenōsis, and divine self-limitation, it clamours for reconstruction and extension.

To read this book even a few weeks after publication is to be greatly surprised by a reality that is vastly different from the target of a great deal of ill-informed criticism and indeed of almost equally ill-informed, sometimes condescending enthusiasm which from its publication this volume has proved to be.

Certainly the essays it contains are written with a measure of passion; there is moreover an underlying, even important consensus between the authors and of course also very considerable differences—witness for example the post-script written by Mr Cupitt or Dr Nineham's epilogue with which the volume ends. There is, however, a central thesis that Professor Hick's team agree in wishing to put forward which they believe very important. It is not an easy thesis to state briefly, partly because the authors are sometimes too scholarly to put it forward baldly, but also because it involves historical, philosophical and theological judgment, in very subtle relation one with another, all of which are disputable. It is indeed a thesis

[1] Revised version of a talk broadcast on Radio 3 on 2nd September 1977, and subsequently repeated.

that I can myself accept as an essay in 'Theologic des Korrektivs', the theology of correction, to borrow Kierkegaard's useful phrase.

In some respects, indeed, I believe the thesis is radically mistaken; but it is not, emphatically not, a denial of Christ's divinity. It might rather be said to be a plea that we liberate the doctrine of Christ's divinity from the 'myth of God incarnate'. But is the Incarnation a myth, and if so in what sense? There is a useful essay in the volume by Professor Wiles which is concerned to distinguish different senses of the word 'myth' on part of which I shall say something later.

'He came down to earth from heaven, who is God and Lord of all.' These words from a very familiar children's Christmas hymn echo the language of the creed: 'who for us men and for our salvation came down from heaven'. The words of the creed in turn echo the word of Paul: 'who, though he was rich, yet for our sakes he became poor'. None of this language is technical; it is much nearer that of 'fairy story', to use a term we shall discuss later. It is certainly a long way from the formidable ontological language of nature (phūsis), substantiality and the rest. And yet according to some of the writers of this book, what happens in the traditional doctrine of the Incarnation is that these crude and indeed moving simplicities are clothed in the sophisticated drapery of the sort of metaphysical story, allegedly widely current in the Hellenistic world into which Christianity had already moved a good twenty years before the Jewish-Roman War of A.D. 70, and in which in fact it took root. This metaphysical story was itself in its own way religious and indeed in some of the ways in which it was told hardly distinguishable from forms of religious mysticism. It was always ultimately Platonic in inspiration, taking over from the Plato of the 'middle dialogues', his supposed vision of a timeless intelligible exemplary world of being on which the world of becoming, disclosed to sense-awareness, asymmetrically depended, and which that world of becoming more or less imperfectly bodied forth.

According to the doctrine of the Incarnation as presented in this book, the Logos, the Word, the eternal Son pre-exists in indissoluble union with God the Father, the Ultimate, the Eternal. Indeed He is of one essential being with that Father in the realm of static perfection. From that realm He issues forth (yet never leaving it), taking to himself manhood in Jesus of Nazareth, yet remaining Himself the subject of that human experience. He lives a human life, he dies a human death, he is raised and exalted. In Him there is achieved a wholly unique union of the eternal and temporal, of the two realms of the heavenly and earthly. This doctrine of the Incarnation, it is claimed, succeeds in converting the life, the teaching, the death, the exaltation of Jesus of Nazareth into an extraordinary metaphysical 'fairy tale' which may indeed once have preserved, but now is calculated only to obscure, the genuinely revelatory character of that life.

Now we must begin by asking whether the doctrine of the Incarnation is properly characterized as the 'myth of God Incarnate'. Is it indeed a judgment on the person of Christ that robs him of his human significance, that converts him in fact into a visitant from another realm? Or when we look more closely at what happened in the intellectual experience of the first century and what continues to happen and is still happening in the Christian world, do we find that that doctrine for all its obvious though often ignored, incompleteness (and I would stress this incompleteness) still represents a tremendous effort (often renewed) to do justice to the belief that in Jesus Christ we have to reckon before all else with a quite unique movement from God to man. 'God was in Christ reconciling the world to himself.' What of the manner of that presence? The doctrine or myth of the Incarnation would claim that in spite of all, we have to reckon here with the reality of divine condescension. Or if that word is loaded (as Mr Cupitt rightly reminds us in his essay that it may be), may we not speak of divine self-limitation, even of a wholly unique act of such divine self-limitation that discloses in a way altogether without parallel God's relation to the world he has created? It discloses that relation in a way without parallel because this act of self-limitation is itself the ground of that relationship.

This act of self-limitation, of kenōsis, as it is often called, is such a disclosure because for Christian faith it is on its accomplishment that a human being's relation to God depends, made what it is by that self-giving. In this act Father, Son and Holy Spirit are all involved; but it is on the Word Incarnate in Jesus of Nazareth that the work is focussed and in his strange, highly individual yet always desperately human career that it reaches its term in defeat, agony and death. To go further would involve us in some of the most tormenting issues of Christian theology, in particular the question how the very unity of the threefold God is as it were put at risk in Jesus' ministry; and while the reality of that risk puts a question mark against the traditional insistence that in God there is no passivity and therefore no possibility of suffering, yet it is part of the achievement of this book that more than one of its essays takes us a little way towards the depths of the cry: 'My God, my God, why hast thou forsaken me?'

'God was in Christ reconciling the world unto himself;' yet the one in whom God was thus asserted to be uniquely active is recorded as saying 'Why callest thou me good? One only is good, namely God'. He is also almost contemptuously dismissive of the sort of adulation that delights in honorific confession, but turns aside from the harder tasks of discipleship. The school of faith indeed in which his closest intimates receive their training is less one of accuracy of theological expression, though it would seem that their conception of the manner of Israel's deliverance had to be radically revised, than of separating pretence from reality in attachment to the way of the Son of Man. 'Simon, Simon, Satan has desired to have you that he may sift you as wheat. However, after you are turned again, strengthen your brethren.' Indeed nothing to me personally is more impressive in this respect than the contrast between the two volumes of Luke's account of Christian origins. In his Gospel, Luke offers a profound presentation of Jesus' life, his pursuit of his Father's business from His visit at the age of twelve to Jerusalem for Passover, to his commendation in death of His spirit to His Father's hands, winning from the centurion acclamation then as an innocent man. Whereas in his second volume, (I speak here for myself) repeatedly one hears the note of a tired ecclesiastical triumphalism anticipating a very great deal that we are more than familiar with in later studies of missionary expansion, almost blandly oblivious of the political context in which the church's work is done. In one of the best essays in the book, that of Mr Cupitt on the Christ of Christendom, later illustrations of this same triumphalist temper are powerfully adduced from the world of Christian art—representation of God, Father, Son and Holy Spirit—and its underlying anthropomorphism is effectively brought out. For its pervasive fault is in the end the refusal to leave the final verdict to God, the seeking after a sign, even when, as in the examples quoted by Mr Cupitt, the signs are of human devising. But while Mr Cupitt rightly draws from his argument the conclusion that Christology must be theocentric, he does not, I think, recognise the extent to which such a Christology also demands, as I have implied above, that the conception of God itself be transformed: the conception of God, that is, in His trancendence. It was indeed just this conception of God in His transcendence that the doctrine of the Incarnation demanded should be reconstructed, even though the classical form of that reconstruction, namely the doctrine of the Trinity, requires close and critical scrutiny, more attention incidentally than it is often given now by writers on what they call the Christian understanding of God.

I must confess, however, that I welcome greatly Mr Cupitt as in fundamental agreement with myself, I hope he will not mind my saying this, in regarding Constantine's so-called conversion in all its consequences as arguably the greatest single disaster in the history of the Christian church.

The authors of these essays are professional theologians and scholars and for that reason their essays should receive the careful and minute appraisal that their quality and their writers' standing demand. Indeed it is worth remarking that two of the essayists—Dr Michael Goulder and Dr Frances Young—are locked in argument with one another over the rôle of the Samaritans in shaping the form of early Christianity. It is just this fact that makes general comment on the book unsatisfactory, this and the fact of which I find myself sharply conscious, that the writers are by no means at ease in handling the history and sense of such notions as substance. Few of them display the sort of technical philosophical expertise which is a necessary condition of proper exploration of the many difficulties attaching to the use of that concept in theology, indeed to the determination of its precise sense. Yet the book demands that anyone who refuses to dismiss the doctrine of Incarnation as 'fairy tale' should defend himself and this is certainly not its least valuable feature.

In his essay on *Myth in Theology* Professor Maurice Wiles surveys the treatment of Christ's temptations in the wilderness in a series of commentaries on Luke's Gospel, beginning with Plummer in the International Critical Commentary in 1910 and going on to very recent work. He indicates in the end his own sympathy with the point of view of the modern editor who finds himself, in his own words, 'in the presence of fairy tale, a typical ancient story on the theme of the testing of the hero.'

I do not myself find Luke's story typical; but that is a relatively minor point. What is more important is that Professor Wiles seems to dismiss out of hand the possibility that we have cast unquestionably in 'mythological' form, (surely another sense of the word 'myth' from 'fairy tale') a recollection of what Jesus himself may have said concerning his own most strenuous self-interrogation, as if he had first to put to himself the question: 'What think you of Christ?' before he could put it to others. It was out of such experience that he learned to say with simple truth that he was among men as a servant and that so and not otherwise he made present to them the ways of His Father.

I spoke a little while back of self-limitation, of kenōsis. There is very clear limitation in any man who has thus to search out for himself the secret of his own significance as something far from immediately obvious or transparent to himself. According to the doctrine of the Incarnation, Christ's self-submission to these conditions is to be seen not as an abdication of divine omnipotence but rather as its only authentic human manifestation. We need to free ourselves from the sort of anthropomorphism that Mr Cupitt so rightly castigates by schooling ourselves to find the secret of God's power there: the secret of that power of which Paul said that it was 'to the Jews a stumbling block and to the Greeks', (including those of the Hellenistic world) 'a foolishness'.

It is indeed by the effectiveness with which it promotes rather than impedes deliverance from such fashioning of the ways of God after a human image that the so-called 'myth of God Incarnate' may recover and sustain its authority. It may recover and sustain its authority because in spite of all it does justice to the unfathomable paradox of the union of the transcendent and the desperately human (so individually human in victory and defeat) that we find in Jesus of Nazareth. It is Jesus of Nazareth who manifests the divine transcendence as present in Himself, in those places in which His human actuality might be thought at first sight most completely to obscure it. 'There stands one among you whom you know not'—So the evangelist for whom Jesus is the Word through whom all things are made.

Chapter 10

THE RELATION OF THE DOCTRINES OF THE INCARNATION AND THE TRINITY

The aim of this paper is not historical; it does not follow the method classically illustrated in Lebreton's well-known study of the origins of the doctrine of the Trinity, still less to duplicate the excellent study not long ago published by my colleague in Cambridge Professor G. C. Stead.[1] What it seeks is perhaps nearer in style to Professor Moltmann's well-known book *Der gekreuzigte Gott*.[2] That book is indeed a work which I greatly admire and I have also had the privilege of discussing part of it with its author. But he would allow me to say that the main lines of what I venture to set out were more or less completely drawn before I read what he had written.

There are in Christian theology a certain number of unresolved problems which touch the very heart of its most fundamental concerns. I say unresolved problems; I might have said rather places where absolutely central issues are clearly at stake, where a whole number of questions seem almost to tumble into one another, and where at the same time, any sort of clarity seems more a matter of fitful vision, than of sustained perception.

There are few better introductions to the questions with which I wish to deal in this paper than a fragment from the notebooks of Gerard Manley Hopkins, belonging to the year of his tertianship:

Why did the Son of God go thus forth from the father not only in the eternal and intrinsic procession of the Trinity but also by

[1] *Theology*, 1974 pp. 508–17, 582–8.
[2] Munich, 1973; ET, London, 1974.

an extrinsic and less than eternal, let us say an aeonian one? To give God glory and that by sacrifice . . . This sacrifice and this outward procession is a consequence and shadow of the procession of the Trinity, from which mystery sacrifice takes its rise; but of this I do not mean to write here. It is as if the blissful agony or stress of selving in God had forced out drops of sweat or blood, which drops were the world, or as if the lights lit at the festival of that 'peaceful Trinity' through some little cranny striking out lit up into being one 'cleave' out of the world of possible creatures. The sacrifice would be the Eucharist . . .[3]

If I was concerned with the interpretation of this very remarkable passage with full regard to its author, I should have to treat of the metaphysics and theology of Duns Scotus, and also of the elusive concept of the *aevum*, introduced by medieval theologians as a kind of middle term between temporal and eternal. But the passage is simply quoted as a point of departure. For surely it conveys with the sort of passion that one would expect from a considerable poet the way in which the two realities of the eternal God and the historical mission of the Incarnate play upon each other. If I may speak very loosely in a way that may seem offensive to the philosophical conscience, it is as if the still transcendence of God in his aseity suddenly became vibrant with the energy, the strain, the joy, the grief, the triumph and the failure of the ministry of Jesus and that ministry itself was found in all its tension and incompleteness to catch in a manner wholly unique the very being of the eternal. The language of my commentary may seem extravagant; certainly it has nothing of the grace of the original. But it is of a coincidence of opposites, an interpenetration of seemingly mutually alien realities that Hopkins writes. By this interpenetration both alike are illuminated.

[3] *The Sermons and Devotional Writings of Gerard Manley Hopkins*, ed. by Christopher Devlin, London, 1967.

What is clear is that the poet's meditation takes for granted the legitimacy of an *ontological* idiom in Christology. In his influential book *Die Christologie des neuen Testaments*,[4] Dr Oscar Cullmann argued that the New Testament titles of Christ were to be construed *functionally*, and not *ontologically*. Where the Johannine self-designations, Light of the World, Bread of Life, Resurrection and Life, Way, Truth and Life etc. were concerned, Cullmann invoked the authority of an interesting monograph on the Johannine Christology[5] published a few years before his own book by Dom Jacques Dupont, OSB. For Cullmann the terms—*ontological* and *functional*—are correlatives; his use of the term *ontological* has little or nothing to do with the branch of philosophy called ontology, by Professor Peter Geach of the University of Leeds, for instance,[6] who in faithfulness to the tradition classically formulated in Aristotle's *Metaphysics*, spoke of it as that branch of philosophy concerned to give as comprehensive account as possible of certain concepts, involved in discourse concerning any subject-matter whatsoever e.g. thing and quality, existence, truth, etc. Such enquiries indeed have great significance of theology, as mention of the conceptual apparatus involved in the Nicence and Chalcedonian definitions reminds us. But when Cullmann referred to *ontological* as distinct from *functional* Christological concepts, he was concerned to distinguish concepts by means of which Christ's work is articulated from concepts purporting to capture what the One is, who in Him is incarnate.

The influence of Melanchthon's well-known dictum: *Hoc est Christum cognoscere, eius beneficia cognoscere* is here strong. For us to know Christ (including in this knowledge an ability to characterize what may be said of him, and not for instance of

[4] Tübingen, 1957; ET, London, 1960.
[5] *Études sur la Christologie de St. Jean*, Paris, 1950.
[6] Proceedings of the Joint Session of the Aristotelian Society and Mind Association, 1951.

Hosea and Jeremiah, of Socrates, of the author of the 2nd Epistle to the Corinthians, of John Bunyan and John Henry Newman, of Dietrich Bonhoeffer and Franz Jägerstätter) is to know the rôle or rôles that is or are exclusively his. What he is apart from such rôle or rôles which help to define the order of his ministry, we do not know, nor need to know. Thus it would seem that the sort of deep theological enquiry undertaken by the late Bishop Frank Weston in his book *The One Christ*[7] would be disallowed as certainly sterile and arguably invalid *ab initio*.

> Verbum supernum prodiens,
> Nec Patris linquens dexteram
> > (St Thomas Aquinas)

It may be said that even thus to pose the question of the relation of the Word incarnate to the Word through whom the entire created order is sustained in being is to be precipitated into every sort of metaphysical bewilderment, and those especially concerning the relations of the temporal to the eternal. Yet according to Dr Alec Vidler, the late Professor C. E. Raven regarded Weston's book as the greatest Christological work in English of this century, and this in spite of the deep differences that separated the two men over such issues as the 'Kikuyu controversy', and the missionary bishop's reaction to the sort of theology he judged encouraged in Oxford by metaphysical idealism on the one hand, and by the attitude to the traditional conciliar orthodoxy encouraged by the *Quellen-forschung* of the synoptic Gospels, characteristic of Sanday's seminar, on the other.[8]

The events that go to make up the history of Jesus belong to

[7] London, 1907.
[8] Yet when Sanday read *The One Christ* he said that he was proud of his 'old pupil'!

the same time order as the conspiracy of Seianus against Tiberius Caesar which was contemporary with some of them. Indeed there are those who argue that Pilate was particularly vulnerable to the suggestion that if he let go one who might be thought to have spoken against Caesar, he could hardly be regarded as Tiberius' friend. (It is alleged of Pilate that he had been involved at least on the fringe of that conspiracy and therefore would wish to avoid even the faintest *soupçon* of disloyalty towards the all-powerful despot on Capri.) The life of Jesus, the last years of Tiberius, the principate of Caligula, the whole complex reality of the Roman world belong to that created order fashioned through the Logos, continually sustained by his power and owing its unity to his creative activity. Further it is not the world of human history alone that finds its ground in the eternal Word, but the natural world in which that history is set, which is itself moreover part of a universe of which in recent decades we have achieved, through empirical cosmology, a greater understanding than any previously possible to human kind. There was no single theological point more continually emphasized by Professor Charles Raven than the total impropriety of treating the natural world and, by implication, the universe, as if they were no more than the stage set for the drama of redemption. He greatly welcomed an article which the late Cardinal Jean Daniélou contributed to *Études* in February 1962 in which he claimed that Teilhard's most important contribution to theology was the administration of a *coup de grâce* to any and every tendency to treat the Christian God as a *deus ex machina*. The Word incarnate in Christ is continually at work. But how then are we to understand the relationship of the apparently datable concentration of his action in the ministry of Jesus, under the circumstances of that period in the history of the society into which he was born and in which he was schooled, to that pervasive continuing activity?

149

The charge is often brought against most forms of kenotic Christology that they fail in the end to make any sense of the relation of the 'depotentiated' Logos incarnate in Jesus to that same Logos eternally and changelessly abiding itself within the unity of the godhead.[9] The duality of the eternal *tropos huparxeōs* and the temporally manifested Logos which seemingly on such a view must be affirmed is dismissed as totally incredible, if not nonsensical.

So inevitably to those who would profess and call themselves orthodox, there was a certain attraction in turning away from the abyss of ontological speculation to the apparent simplicities of a theology that would insist that its fundamental categories were economic, in the sense of being embedded in the structure of the economy of God's dealings with us. The very conception of God as Father, Son, and Holy Spirit must be construed as a conception of God in his relation to his creatures in creation, redemption, and sanctification.

Yet as we well know, such a view has failed in fact to sustain itself for more than a very short period. The reasons for this failure are several. I should like immediately to focus on one of them, and paradoxical though it may seem, I should like to suggest that I find this very powerfully indicated in Bultmann's great commentary on the fourth Gospel.[10] (I realize that this must appear paradoxical, in view, for instance, of the form of Cullmann's acute criticism of Bultmann's depreciation of the sacramental teaching of that Gospel.) In his commentary, affected as it is by his study of Kierkegaard, Bultmann powerfully brings out the extent to which radically Christocentric though John's Gospel is, that Christocentrism is

[9] Cf. J. M. Creed, *The Divinity of Jesus Christ*, ed. by D. M. MacKinnon (Fontana), London, 1964.

[10] London, 1971. The reader will realize that my debt is to Bultmann's theological exegesis and not to the *Quellen-forschung* which his commentary also contains.

parasitic upon a continued reference to the Father who sent the Son, which gives the book its ultimately theocentric emphasis. It is not Jesus who himself imposes significance on what he is and does; rather he continually advertises the fact that his significance lies in this, that it is wholly bestowed upon him *ab extra*. In Bultmann's own theological thought the central emphasis is always epistemological. 'Jesus reveals that He is the revealer.' His import is found in that God is uniquely disclosed through him, in his own preaching and then in the preaching which has him as its subject. Yet if Jesus is to reveal that 'He is the revealer', thus disclosing that his significance is not in himself, and that where he is concerned, the most important fact is this, that he is the identifiable historical individual through whom God has addressed the world, we may claim that this is only possible through the realization in his historical individuality of a total receptivity.

And here I quote another student of the fourth Gospel, of a very different temper from Bultmann, namely Dr W. R. Inge. In his oddly entitled study *Faith and its Psychology*,[11] he speaks of an 'infinite self-abnegation' as characteristic of the Johannine Christology. His idiom is ontological. Clearly he takes very seriously John's suggestion that what is realized in the Incarnate Word's earthly ministry is properly characterized as the achievement of such a total self-abnegation. Indeed he encourages his readers to ask themselves how far that which is incarnate in Jesus may not be characterized as infinite receptivity, infinite response. Few would deny that for John, the Word is pre-existent, even if in that sentence we are in fact saying (this is Cullmann's view) that what pre-exists is that to which *we* refer by the 'definite description', the Word.[12] That

[11] London, 1909.
[12] For Cullmann the designation 'Word of God' refers to Jesus in his relation to us. On the relation of 'Word' and 'Son' in the Johannine theology, the

which is represented as coming into the world in Jesus, as transcribed in the conditions of his ministry into forms of speaking his Father's words and 'doing the will of Him that sent me', is what he eternally is.

It was an Italian prior who spoke somewhere of obedience as 'the most insidious' (the Italian word is *subdola*) of all the temptations. This characterization of obedience was certainly one of the most illuminating contributions to fundamental Christian ethics I have heard in years. But it is not only for Christian ethics that it is important; it is also deeply significant for dogmatic theology, both for soteriology and for the doctrine of God. The direction of the argument in the preceding paragraphs may have seemed to suggest that in Jesus we find a total obedience to the will of God. And of course the New Testament gives a certain encouragement in that direction, e.g. (a *locus classicus*), 'obedient unto death', Philippians 2.1ff. Yet Paul says first that he made himself of no reputation (*doxa*). He implies a complete indifference to human judgement which is expressive not of a strenuous heroism, but of a total self-abandonment to the Father. Thus in the *third* Gospel the young Jesus chides his parents, who seek him after Passover, with the words that he must be in his Father's house, about his Father's business, and the dying man, the temptation to prove himself to himself and to the world at large finally resisted by refusal to descend from the Cross, utters as his last word: 'Father into thy hands I commend my spirit.' It is only after that last word that the centurion in charge of the execution squad confesses him an innocent man (*dikaios*). Yet it is his refusal to attempt descent from the Cross that enables him to receive the 'penitent thief's' confession of faith.[13] So, as Barth so clearly saw, Jesus is 'the man

posthumous study of the late Dr. W. H. Cadman – *The Open Heaven* – (Blackwell) is very valuable.

[13] It is very important that in his account of Jesus' temptations, Luke finds the climactic temptation not in the offer of the Kingdoms of this world and

for others' in so far as he is 'the man for God'. Because his very costly, total indifference to human judgement is grounded in a loving self-abandon to his Father, it makes possible for him an analogous accessibility to the outcast and derelict.

A man's conduct may sometimes be excused on the ground that he was obeying orders. Whether that conduct is good or bad in itself and/or by reason of its consequences is what determines whether or not we should approve it. No one would question the heroism of the German soldiers at Stalingrad in 1942; I trust that no one either would question the moral superiority of the action of the Munich students who that same terrible autumn, courted death by open protest against the monstrous evil the soldiers were sustaining by their brave obedience, or of Franz Jägerstätter in his solitary witness to death as an Austrian CO the next August.

If we find the starting-point of a Christology in the relation of Christ to the Father, realized for our salvation in flesh and blood, we have to recognize that what is thus realized is in itself an ultimate gentleness of receiving and of giving back, even of parting asunder and of accepted estrangement. My language here is anthropomorphic, and perilously nearly tritheistic. Yet the doctrine of the Trinity, of the essential as distinct from the economic Trinity, represents in part at least a grave attempt to

their glory, but in the suggestion Jesus test his status *vis-à-vis* his Father by a descent from the pinnacle of the Temple. The devil then leaves him *achri kairou* to return in the hour of the power of darkness, to enter into Judas, to sift Peter as wheat, and above all to renew his challenge to Jesus to prove himself. Luke's narrative of the Passion is one of a final overwhelming temptation, and that temptation reaches its climax in the challenge to descend from the Cross, the axis of Luke's treatment of the crucifixion. Such a descent, if successfully executed, would have vindicated Jesus' claim, but at a cost totally destructive of his mission. For a more extended treatment of this topic, may I refer to my paper on the evangelical imagination in the volume—*Religious Imagination*, edited by Professor J. P. Mackey, in honour of Professor John McIntyre (Edinburgh University Press, 1986)?

prevent the doctrine of Christ's passion and work from lapsing into a saga of human achievement, or worse still, into that of a demigod, akin to Heracles. It is to engage in the task of so reconstructing the doctrine of the Ultimate that the form of Jesus' ministry, his life, his death, and his being brought again from death to boundless life,[14] is found in God as He is in Himself. At the heart of that ministry we find realized a final, a haunting receptivity. Yet that receptivity never rots away into a passive acceptance. It is not only that, for instance, the temple is cleansed; it is rather that tragic failure in the circumstances of Jesus' mission is characterized for what it is, 'Oh Jerusalem, Jerusalem'. 'Daughters of Jerusalem, weep not for me, but for yourselves.' The situation is not mastered, nor is it accepted; it is lived through and met by agony. We cannot say too often that Jesus failed in very much, even as Antigone in Sophocles' tragedy failed in her confrontation with Creon, bringing out the very worst in that self-conscious ruler. Of that failure Jesus bore the burden, but not in the mood of a ferocious, exultant self-denial; rather as expressive of an identification in love at one with those with whom He was involved, and with the One in relationship to whom is constituted eternally what He is. 'And the spirit drove him into the wilderness.' The theme of the Holy Spirit's role in the mission of the Incarnate needs much further treatment, if this picture is to be, I will not say, complete but tolerably adequate.

So I must turn briefly to the central enigma of the relation of the times of Jesus to the eternity of God. For it is in a proper understanding of this relation that it may be we shall find the key to the problem of the relation of the Word through which the world comes to be and the Word Incarnate in Jesus.

What is realized in the mission of Jesus and perfected in the Father's raising Him from the dead is the very unity of God, the

---

[14] i.e. life no longer moving to the frontier of death.

consistency of God with himself in relation to his creation. We have to do with a prolonged human action that is grounded in God, that in fact provides the very rationale of creation itself. Yet it is unique because in it the very being of God is put at risk, and by the way in which it thus is put at risk, we learn, as nowhere else, what it is we *say* of God when we acclaim him all-powerful, all-knowing, etc. It is a weakness of the western Trinitarian tradition so to conceive and so to stress the unity of God that the whole theology of the divine attributes tends to be treated independently of the treatise on the divine tri-unity, and the unity of God itself regarded as conceivable independently of the tri-unity through which it is realized:

'The hands are stretched in weakness, not in power.'

So Archbishop William Dalrymple Maclagan in a Good Friday hymn,[15] a good deal better than most. But he is wrong. It is the power of God that we must learn to define by reference to those outstretched hands. For we are not passing through the hour of a temporary *eclipse* of the divine sovereignty where we are concerned. We are witnessing its supreme assertion in the setting of a deeply estranged world, an assertion that discloses its very substance, its arcane ground. Our images of the divine are always perilously suffused with anthropomorphic suggestions of a consummate mastery of the world. One catches an example in the prayer that speaks of God as 'high and mighty King of Kings and Lord of Lords', a magnified Henrican-style despot 'without body, parts or passions'. But the divine crown is one of thorns: 'Has he diadem as monarch etc.' One could say that the writer of that hymn[16] (hardly heard today) was (possibly

---

[15] A. & M. Hymn 115, *Lord when thy Kingdom comes*.

[16] *Art thou weary, art thou languid?* It is the translation of a Greek original by Dr J. M. Neale: but in the form of Hymns A. & M. 254, a very paradigm of Victorian hymnody!

unknown to himself) nearer the heart of the matter than the composer of the prayer!

It is only through the reinforcement of our Christology by a profoundly probing doctrine of the essential Trinity that the former is preserved from the sort of distortion which immediately in one way or another, overtakes any attempt to develop an autonomous and all-inclusive doctrine of Christ's person and work, as if both person and work alike could stand on their own feet. It is again only through such a doctrine that the full significance of Christ's revelation may be glimpsed from afar, and the sort of trivialization of the divine that finds expression in succeeding styles of idolatry avoided. If in such effort we often find ourselves reduced to silence by inability to eliminate apparent contradiction from the concepts we invoke, at least we may hope that this silence reflects disturbed movement towards, rather than comforting escape from, God's unutterable love.

It is a commonplace of the histories of the doctrine of the Trinity to contrast the Western emphasis on unity expressed e.g. in the Augustinian invocation of psychological analogies in treatment of persons and processions, with the Greek (Cappadocian) preoccupation with the three *hypostaseis*. Yet we do well to remember that it is fully in accordance with orthodox tradition to insist both that: *Omnia opera Dei ad extra sunt opera totius indivisae Trinitatis* and that: *Missiones sequuntur Processiones.*

Thus the grounds of the rôles *quoad nos* of Son and Spirit are found in their processional relations within the Godhead. And (if I understand Aquinas' treatise *de Trinitate* aright) these relations are to be *identified* with the individual persons. At the outset of his two volume study of the history of Trinitarian doctrine de Régnon[17] illuminatingly suggests that the 'egoism'

---

[17] *Études sur l'histoire du Dogme de la Trinité, vol. 1.* See Appendix C at the end of this essay for a transcription of the passage referred to.

(in the sense of 'I'ness) of the three persons is exhausted in the relation in which that person eternally stands to his fellows. So the 'I'ness of the Son is the relation of Sonship in which he stands to the Father; what he is, is his eternal generation from and response to the Father. So with the Holy Spirit (though here the controversy of the *Filioque* must be treated), his being resides in his being 'co-spired' by Father and Son, posited in and through their mutual relationship; for him to exist as Holy Spirit is *co-spirari*.

To work this out in full use would have to be made of the treatment in modern ontology (beginning with such works as Russell's *Principles of Mathematics* and Moore's famous essay on *Internal and External Relations*) of different sorts of relations, e.g., *transitive, intransitive, symmetrical, asymmetrical, ancestral*, etc. It is notorious that in Aquinas' treatise *de Trinitate* the frontiers between substance, and relation are blurred. The relations with which the persons of the Trinity are identified are characterized as quasi-substantial. But the notion of substance which the early Church theologians invoked, e.g. in treatment of the identity of deity when predicated of Father and Son, was partly useful to them in treatment of totally novel problems because the *aporia*, which remained after Aristotle's sustained and subtle 'exploration of its veins and sinews' (the phrase is that of the late Dom David Knowles, OSB), suggested a fluidity or 'openness of texture' in the notion that made it unexpectedly useful in articulation of unprecedented problems.[18] But what is true of

[18] On this may I refer to my two essays—Aristotle's *Conception of Substance* in *New Essays in Plato and Aristotle*, London, 1965, and *Substance in Christology* in *Cambridge Essays in Christology*, Cambridge, 1972? See also J. M. Le Blond: *Logique et Méthode chez Aristote*, Paris, and various essays in the *Festschrift* for Monsignor A. Mansion: *Autour d'Aristote*, Louvain, 1962. For a different view, see the important study of Aristotle by Professor G. E. M. Anscombe in the volume: *Three Philosophers* by Professors Anscombe and Geach, (Blackwell, 1962).

the notion of substance will be found to apply analogously to that of relation.

Yet already I can imagine impatience with this apparent attempt to substitute for the Gospel of God a 'bloodless ballet of impalpable' abstractions. It is as if the *saltus de Christo ad Deum trinum* is a leap not into the abyss but into a world in which dexterity in handling fundamental notions in philosophical logic, and the adjacent territory of ontology (in Geach's sense) takes over from reverence and from humanity. Whereas what is imposed on us is a new dimension of the perennial work of faith seeking understanding.

Yet it is an inescapable aspect of theological existence as we know it, continually to encounter this paradox, viz. that is, if we refuse the philistine and spiritually distorting amputation of our theological reach that must be our lot if we accept Cullmann's restriction as finally authoritative. (We must remember that Karl Barth, for all his Christocentrism, or even Christomonism, will have nothing of it.) And here inevitably I refer again to my remark that God's consistency with himself, his very unity, is at risk in the ministry and expecially the Passion of Jesus.

My debt here to the work of Hans Urs von Balthasar is very great. As I remarked in an article I contributed to the *Clergy Review* in 1969, there are few (if any) living theologians from whom I have learnt and continue to learn more. In particular his essay, *Mysterium Paschale*[19] in the composite *Mysterium Salutis* III 2 (ed. Feiner and Löhrer) has been constantly in my mind. This very dense monograph dares to treat the unity of the Triune

---

[19] An expanded version of this article has appeared as an introduction to the translation of von Balthasar's *Engagement with God* by Dr J. Halliburton, London, 1975. The interested student is referred to the excellent study of von Balthasar by Mr John Riches in *Theology* for 1972, and to the volume of essays—*The Theology of Beauty* (T. & T. Clark, 1986), which includes a more extended treatment of von Balthasar's Christology, as presented in his later major work *Theodramatik*.

God, the very consistency of God with Himself, as something needing affirmation in relation to the creation. It is as if that unity were not an eternal self-sufficiency, a transcendent and formally complete wholeness, but something which because its eternal realization is in and through the perpetual mutuality of the processions of the Three comprising it, may find itself at risk by the predicament of its creation, and by the cost exacted for that creation's fulfilment by reason of that predicament. It is as if the theology of the Triune God, understood as a completion of the theology of Christ's *kenōsis* and the complex simplicity of his redeeming mission, provided the context within which traditional debates concerning the alleged divine passibility, or impassibility are transformed. God is transcendent in the sense that the world's dependence upon Him is totally asymmetrical. Yet in Himself He is such that the very dependence of the world upon Him is expressive of his eternal relatedness. The creator's humility before his creature is the centrepoint of the mystery of the divine humility, which is the very ground of the divine omnipotence. That power in its absolute sovereignty must not be conceived abstractly but in terms of the total and unfettered *perichoresis* of the persons. Indeed the humility of God may be identified with the Son as response to the Father *in vinculo Spiritus*.

If Raven was right in insisting that we must not treat the natural universe as the stage-set for the drama of redemption, so surely also was Oliver Quick when in private conversation with myself in the autumn of 1941, he said that he regarded as the very touchstone of orthodoxy the frankly mythological clause in the Creed—*descendit de coelis*. Quick was no pre-Copernican! Yet he insisted that this dramatic, mythological idiom was irreducible, the point at which the perennial search on the part of Christianity for a metaphysic in which to rest came to an end. The search had continually to be made if only to bring out more effectively the irreducible surd of the movement of God to men.

Yet what is the doctrine of the Trinity if not the effort so to reconstruct the doctrine of God that this 'descent' may be seen as supremely, indeed paradigmatically, declaratory of what He is in himself? That God is ultimate humility, a selflessness that in the life of the Incarnate shows itself in a total indifference to the survival of 'institutional Christianity' if only the Father's truth may be affirmed redemptively for those 'lost sheep' to whom he came (cf. again the refusal to descend from the Cross)—these are strange, paradoxical truths: yet they may be arguably more easily perceived by a Church that must seek to redefine its *moyen d'être*, and in consequence made receptive of its *raison d'être* as the embodiment of Christ's sheerly precarious existence, in the new freedom of its post-Constantinian age. Because the built-in institutional carapace of the Christian reality (as we have known it) is being destroyed, we are coming to see that the concepts of the divine sovereignty, and the kingship of Christ must be schematized anew. Only this re-schematization calls not for a facile self-dispensation from the burden of metaphysical thought, but rather for a deeper, because less artificially protected, engagement with its relation to the representation of Christ's reality.

It is paradoxical that at a time when there is great interest in the characteristically Christian doctrine of God, it is by no means uncommon for this interest to be accompanied by a certain impatience with the doctrine of the Trinity. Yet it remains true that the history of this doctrine represents the most sustained effort made to reconstruct the conception of the Absolute under the central conviction that the mission of Jesus (and here we include his resurrection and the coming upon his disciples of the Holy Spirit) is, in an altogether unique sense, the actuality of the divine self-impartation to the world. It is a commonplace to point out that how far removed the ontological categories, by which the Chalcedonian definition sought by the concept of hypostatic union to affirm the irreducible uniqueness of the union of ultimately incommensurables is from the simplicities of Galilee; in the doctrine of the Trinity, whether one attends to the tradition classically articulated by the Cappadocians or to the Latin concentration on the divine unity, we find ourselves involved in the use of the same notions—of substance, of property, of relation etc. But even a writer, as traditional as de Régnon, is firmly emphatic that whatever is said *de Deo Trino* is said *analogice*, and in analogy the way of *negation* is always sovereign over that of *eminence*. To claim otherwise is to plunge into the sort of anthropomorphism that involves either an almost overt tritheism or an ultimately monadic conception of the divine mind mitigated only by the sly introduction into the characterization of its activity, of the concepts of different intellectual dispositions which though very properly distinguished in analysis of human awareness, can hardly be extrapolated to the level of the divine without the most rigorous qualification.

What remains, however, unquestionably true, and this is a central thesis of this essay, is that the doctrine of the Trinity has to a very considerable extent been developed out of properly considered relation to the unresolved issues pertaining to the relation of time to God. Here the quotation from Hopkins' *Notebooks* at the outset of the paper was deliberately included to advertise the cruciality of this question. The conception of kenōsis is emphatically (in my judgment) the conception which alone enables us to approach the *arcana* of the divine condescension. It is a conception which is traditional in that it regards the pre-existence of the Word or Son as essential to a valid Christology. It is of course a part of the doctrine of the Trinity to suggest (it can do no more) concerning the manner of that pre-existence, to indicate the eternal relationship that is constitutive of it in so far as it is the pre-existence of a distinguishable person whose distinguishable uniqueness can easily be lost sight of in the torrential energy of the Deity, in the mutual interpenetration of its constitutent persons: energy that is at one and the same time expressive of a total spontaneity and absolute mutual response. Yet within the context of this totally uninhibited, but triadic aseity, we have to reckon with the actuality of limit, of *peras* or boundary. It is through this actuality that, for instance, the *idiotēs* of the Son as eternal receptivity is constituted, a receptivity that in the manner of the Incarnate life is expressed in his dependence, realized in the form of his human submission in respect of the hour of his agony and his glorification, and also in the role of the Spirit Who within his history is presented as effective in the order of his coming and going, but Whom he is also enabled to bestow upon his disciples in the setting of his glorification.[20]

If we suppose that in the theology of the Trinity an *analogia personarum* can be completed by an analogy of *limits* (in the pregnant sense of the Greek *peras*), it may go some way towards grounding within the eternal, the essentially human element of temporality, the sense of inescapable limitation. For this element of temporality (clearly dependent, as it is, upon awareness of temporal direction as a cosmological ultimate) belongs to the substance of Jesus' comings and goings. What it was for him to be human was to be subject to the sort of fragmentation of effort, curtailment of design, interruption of purpose, distraction of resolve that belongs to temporal experience. To leave one place for another is to leave work undone; to give attention to one suppliant is to ignore another; to expend energy today is to leave less for tomorrow. We have to ask ourselves how far this very conformity to the complex discipline of temporality, this acceptance of the often tragic consequences

---

[20] One recalls how very clearly in John 20 the revelation of the risen Lord and the bestowal of Holy Spirit are integrated: indeed deep analysis of that chapter suggests that for the fourth Evangelist, the separate events of Easter, Ascension Day and Pentecost are presented as in fact falling within twenty-four hours, aspects of the single Paschal mystery.

that spring from its obstinate, ineluctable truncation of human effort, belongs to the very substance of Jesus' defeat. Jesus' acceptance of this part of his burden can arguably be interpreted as a painfully realized transcription into the conditions of our existence, of the receptivity, the defined, even if frontierless, receptivity that constitutes his person. It is indeed as that which makes such transcription possible that we must first see the divine relation to the temporal. It is a relation that we will misunderstand except we see the God so related as triune.

APPENDIX A

Cullman & Bultmann

In fairness to Dr Cullmann, it should be remembered that in his last major work—*Heil als Geschichte*, Tübingen, 1966,—he offered a penetrating and sustained criticism of the radical subjectivism that may be judged the central blemish of the theological interpretation of the New Testament by Rudolf Bultmann, and some of his followers, but still more by Professor John Knox. Granted that with the wide influence of the work of such theologians as Wolfhart Pannenberg and Jürgen Moltmann (and the latter's early deep indebtedness to the independent Marxism of Ernst Bloch has understandably proved effective as a liberation from an excessive servitude to the metaphysical studies of Martin Heidegger whether in his *Sein und Zeit*, or in his often very interesting later work), the attraction of the sort of radical subjectivism, which surely reaches its *reductio ad absurdum*, in the excursions into general theology by the much admired New York *Neutestamentler*, John Knox, has declined, it still remains true that Cullmann's contribution in *Heil als Geschichte* to the central theological issue of the last two decades is very valuable. He is indeed very self-consciously a theologian who seeks to eschew any involvement in metaphysical discussion, and in the hostages which in this connexion he is prepared to give to fortune, Bultmann has the edge on him. Yet in his argument against Bultmann, one catches quite clearly the vibration within theology proper, of the unresolved metaphysical controversy between idealism or constructivism and realism. (On this issue see especially Michael Dummett: *Frege: Philosophy of Language*, London, 1973, and his Henriette Herz Lecture before the British Academy in the same year: *The Justification of Deduction*, Oxford, 1973.) In conclusion it might be remarked that a comment on Moltmann's truly profound essay *Der gekreuzigte Gott* from a theologian sensitive to the significance for specifically theological issues of the idealist-realist debate might be of considerable value.

APPENDIX B

Küng on Divine Impassiblity

It is a weakness of Hans Küng's *Menschwerdung Gottes*, (Herder, 1970), that after his very lengthy survey of Hegel's treatment of Christological themes, in a full and impressive chapter devoted to criticism, in the light of lessons extracted from his previous study of the notion of divine impassibility, he largely averts from the Trinitarian issues to which inevitably his concentration on Hegel's characteristic theological emphases had directed his attention. The chapter that follows the treatment of impassibility is devoted to an informed, but strangely flaccid and pedestrian, survey of the 'old' and 'new' quests for the historical Jesus. It is a useful summary, and a part-indication of its acknowledged and unacknowledged hostility to the traditional treatises *de Verbo Incarnato*. But it lacks any clear conclusion and is intellectually unsatisfying. Only in the last appendix of his very long work, inspired partly by von Balthasar's *Mysterium Paschale* to treat of Kenosis, does Küng show how he might have converted to most valuable use his brilliantly impressionistic, and admittedly often vulnerable, presentation of Hegel's *oeuvre* in grounding theologically his rejection of the traditional concept of impassibility in the doctrine of the Trinity, thus indeed showing the way in which the deep insights it enshrines, excellently caught in the late Dr J. K. Mozley's classical monograph on the theme, but also admitted by a theologian as different in temper as the late Dr Niebuhr in his Gifford Lectures, might be reconciled with a proper sensitivity to the concrete actuality of the Incarnate.

APPENDIX C

From *Études de Théologie positive sur La Sainte Trinité* by Th. de Régnon, SJ, Vol. 1, Paris, 1892, pp. 67/f

I II SECTION 7

Mais gardons-nous de pousser trop loin cette assimilation, de peur qu'elle n'égare notre pensée. Après avoir constaté les ressemblances, voyons les dissemblances. Saint Damascène nous signale la principale: 'Les hypostases crées, dit-il, sont isolées et non les unes dans les autres ... En la sainte Trinité, tout le contraire ... les hypostases sont les unes dans les autres, ἐν ἀλλήλαις γαρ αἱ ὑποστάσεις εἰσιν.'[21] Sans entrer encore dans l'étude de cette métaphysique, éclairons-nous à sa lumière.

La personne humaine est inclinée à tout rapporter à soi, et à se rapporter à soi-même. Je ne décide pas si c'est là une nécessité constitutive ou une défectuosité vicieuse. Mais il reste que bien

---

[21] S. Damascène, *Foi orthod.*, liv. I, ch. VIII.–M. col. 828 et 829.

des vices résultent de cette tendance: orgueil, ambition, jalousie, avarice; toutes passions se résumant en un seul mot: *égoïsme*. Par état, le moi est possesseur, je l'accorde; mais, par abus, il devient accapareur; facilement il repousse et exclut le non-moi. Encore un coup, la personne humaine tend à rapporter à soi et sa propre nature et tout le reste.

Hé bien! de la personne divine concevez tout le contraire. Les théologiens en donnent une définition qui semble un paradoxe. Chaque personne divine, distent-ils, est une *relation subsistante*. Expression étrange, puisque, d'après les idées communes, rein n'est moins substance qu'une relation. Mais cette définition a pour but de nous enseigner que, de même que dans une relation chaque terme se rapporte à son corrélatif, de même chaque personne divine, bien que subsistant dans l'identité de la substance infinie, se rapporte tout entière à une autre personne.

Qui dit: 'père', dit: 'père d'un fils'.—Qui dit: 'fils', dit: 'fils d'un père'. Être père, c'est avoir un fils; être fils, c'est avoir un père. Je sais que parmi les hommes la paternité est quelque chose de surajouté, car l'homme est constitué personne humaine, avant qu'il ne soit père. Mais en Dieu toute la personnalité du Père consiste dans la paternité. Tout entier il est père, et par conséquent sa personne tout entière se rapporte à son Fils. A son tour, le Fils n'est pas autre chose que fils au point de vue personnel, et par conséquent sa personne tout entière se rapporte à son Père.

Oh! que sont bien choisis ces noms de Père et de Fils! Ou plutôt que Dieu a été bon et sage, en créant la paternité humaine pour nous permettre de concevoir quelque chose de la Paternité divine! Voyez comme un bon père se penche vers son fils pour se déverser en lui, et comme un bon fils se tourne vers son père pour se rapporter à lui. La gloire du père est son fils, l'honneur du fils est son père.

O mon âme! abandonne-toi à ces nobles pensées. Oublie les égoïsmes humains pour contempler les égoïsmes divins.

Conçois, si tu le peux, un père qui ne soit que père, un fils qui ne soit que fils. Tout l'égoïsme de ce père consiste à donner à son fils toute la substance de ses richesses: *Pater diligit Filium et omnia dedit in manu ejus.*[22] Tout l'égoïsme du fils est de se rapporter à son père, soi-même et tout le reste, afin que soi-même et tout le reste accomplisse la volonté du père; *non quaero voluntatem meam, sed voluntatem ejus qui misit me.*[23] Encore une fois, le propre d'un tel père est de tout donner à son fils; le propre d'un tel fils est de tout rendre à son père; *et mea omnia tua sunt et tua mea sunt.*[24]

Telle est la manière dont nous devons concevoir une personne divine. Que cette lumière du coeur nous éclaire et nous échauffe, dans la discussion où nous allons reprendre la question d'une façon plus philosophique.

---

[22] John, III, 35.
[23] John, V, 30.
[24] John, XVII, 10.

Chapter 11

PROLEGOMENA TO CHRISTOLOGY

Where the Incarnation is concerned, according to traditional Christian teaching, we have to do with that which is alleged to be unique. The term—*the* Incarnation—is a definite description, the function of the definite article in the phrase expressing it being that of indicating uniqueness of reference. That to which we refer as *the* Incarnation takes place once for all; but what is it for such an event to take place? Indeed what are we saying when we speak of it as an event? Here is focussed the question of the relation of the temporal to the eternal, of man to God, of Christ to God.

Historical events, for instance the premiership of Neville Chamberlain, are unique; unique in the sense of occurring within a particular region of space at a particular time, standing within identifiable relations of contemporaneity, anteriority, and posteriority to other events, etc. They may also be qualitatively unique: in that we say of many such events that nothing precisely or even vaguely like this has happened before, or will happen again. Such events as Chamberlain's premiership are of course inherently complex, and when we speak of their qualitative uniqueness, the quality to which we refer is a *Gestaltqualität* or pattern-quality such as, to take a simple example, we find in a melody. (*Gestaltqualitäten* may have one and only one instance.)

We look indeed for analogies; but in the sort of case I have advanced, we take care lest the analogies confuse us, or blunt the precision of our understanding. Thus we call such action as that of Anthony Blunt treasonable; but in what precise sense is it so characterized? Are we simply bracketing it with, for instance, the activities of Jacobites north and south of the Border in the first decades of the eighteenth century? Surely not; for the differences are enormous between the sort of treasonable activity in which Blunt engaged, and that to which adherents of the Old and Young Pretender committed themselves. Any account of Blunt's treason which sought to lay bare in what it consisted would have to determine what it was that differentiated its character from that of innumerable other instances of treasonable behaviour. Yet while such scrutiny would most certainly reveal at least a part of its uniqueness, that uniqueness would not be such as to make it absolutely unique in the very special sense of its being impossible for us to conceive of its being repeated. And this obscure impossibility we tentatively suppose to be found in the coming of Christ in virtue of the fact that *the* Incarnation (if indeed the description has application) refers to that event in which the whole relation of temporal to eternal is rooted.

If we speak then of the Incarnation as event, we are doing much more than claim for it the sort of qualitative uniqueness or singularity we may claim for Chamberlain's premiership or Blunt's treason. Yet we should not neglect the very serious attempts that have been made to render the problem of this uniqueness less intolerably difficult, its sheerly mysterious character more nearly perspicuous, by reducing or seeking to reduce the difference hitherto stressed. An argument developed (for instance) in Dr B. H. Streeter's essay *Reality*[1] sought to present Jesus of Nazareth as the master of a characteristically religious approach to the world, as a supreme, even as *the* supreme, religious genius, occupying a place, fulfilling a rôle akin to that which we might assign in literature to William Shakespeare, or in music to Johann Sebastian Bach. The one belongs to sixteenth/seventeenth-century England, the latter to eighteenth century Germany. Neither is, in any sense, *déraciné*:

[1] Macmillan, 1927.

both are indebted for their formation to the world in which they grew up and lived. In an unpublished paper, written a few years before his death in 1945, on creativity and determinism, the late Professor A. E. Taylor remarked that although any knowledgeable contemporary observer might have predicted that sooner or later William Shakespeare would turn his hand to writing a revenge tragedy, even that he would draw on the Hamlet cycle, none would have successfully predicted (as an astronomer a transit of Venus) that he would make of the work the Hamlet we know. And this, even if our supposed student enjoyed the kind of privileged access to the writer's psyche, and capacity to read the signs present in his previous work, claimed by Dr Ernest Jones in his strangely haunting *Hamlet and Oedipus*.[2] The originality of genius lies in the power to create what is instantly arresting, out of materials provided by inheritance, environment, personal experience. So (according to this view) in religion with Jesus of Nazareth. It should be emphasized that while Schleiermacher found the religious supremacy of Jesus to reside in the unique depth at which he realized that *Abhängigkeitsgefühl* in which for him religion was essentially comprised, Streeter, as his work in the field of Christian origins attests, was by no means indifferent to the particularity of circumstance where the life of Christ was concerned. If he saw the story of Jesus' career as a Platonic myth (a myth, that is, after the manner of the myth of Gyges in *Republic* ii or that of Er in *Republic* x) with the immense advantage of being a factual record, and not a brilliantly conceived imaginative projection of that which defied conceptual formulation by discursive human intelligence, that factuality only fulfilled for us the conditions required of it, if much of its detail possessed historical verisimilitude. 'The shades of night are already gathering.' When the *chef d'œuvre* of

[2] Gollancz, 1949.

Streeter's work as a *Neutestamentler*, *The Four Gospels*,[3] was published, the Oxford tradition of 'source-criticism' of which it was the definitive expression was already (unnoticed by its continuing practitioners) submitted to the radical critique implicit in the developing 'form-criticism' of the German schools. Yet however precarious in foundation or shallow in hermeneutical perception, the 'Proto-Luke' or 'Four-Document' hypotheses may seem to be, we must credit the man who proposed them with a deep eagerness to restore the historical actuality of our picture of Jesus of Nazareth in order that its profoundly revelatory significance might be secured.

But if it is uniqueness of this sort (viz. uniqueness as supreme master of a religious response to the world) that we find in Jesus, it is a uniqueness that is relative, not absolute. The claim that is made for his uniqueness in this respect is one that is defended by judgement of comparison with others finding their niche, as it were, on a graded scale. Here the reader is presented with a norm in the way in which a literary critic may offer him a canon after the manner of the late Dr. F. R. Leavis treating of the English novel, successively in *The Great Tradition* (1951), in *D. H. Lawrence—Novelist* (1955), and (with his wife) in *Dickens the Novelist* (1970), modifying, even to the point of retractation where Dickens is concerned, his judgement, but all the while enabling a paradigm to emerge by reference to which a great deal of other work may be evaluated, including of course the inferior products of the writers he thinks have contributed to the establishment of the great tradition. So analogously on this view with Jesus: 'author and perfecter' not merely of 'our faith', but by the creativity of his finished achievement, the architect and the builder of a spiritual temple for all mankind. That the temple shall prove indeed a house of prayer for all nations it is for the Spirit, that 'other advocate' which the Father will send in

[3] Macmillan, 1924.

his name, to assure. But in so far as the Spirit takes of the things that are of Jesus and discloses their inmost sense to his disciples, it is his role at once to perpetuate and to extend beyond the frontiers of natural anticipation the diverse richness of the Master's vision. Thus the creativity in Jesus is at once his personal work, and is enabled, as it were, as part of its invisible fruit, to transcend the temporal and geographical, the social, cultural, and historical frontiers of its first expression. This, although the exquisite and hard-wrought innocence, the mysterious and costing purity of its initial embodiment in him must remain as the 'light of the world' come into the world 'not to judge the world, but that through him the world might be saved'; yet 'here is the judgement of this world: now is the Prince of this world cast out'.

But is this uniqueness which we have sought to capture by extended analogy the uniqueness which according to traditional Christian theology, there has been in the Incarnation of the Word of God? Is this the uniqueness predicated of the event of his coming, the action of his life? And the answer is surely *no*. One might begin by suggesting that we have to reckon here with a uniqueness of relation, which is a category of being. We move from a level in which we treat of achievement in a particular human domain, that of religion in contradistinction from that, for example, of the visual or plastic arts, to that of ontology, where the concepts which we employ, and on which we must reflect, are those of the highest possible level of generality, such that we say we encounter them in discourse concerning any subject-matter whatsoever; such concepts as thing and quality, existence, causality, relation, etc.

What can we say of this allegedly unique relation, what of the terms that it relates? Is it a conceivable relation of relata, conceivable, even if it can be understood free of self-contradiction? It is often said that even if the definition of the Council of Chalcedon did not reveal 'the bankruptcy of patristic thought' (William Temple's phrase), in affirming this union of the incommensurables, it simply advertised work to be done, the setting of a question rather than the finding of a solution. Yet it was clearly affirmed that of this union, it is God who is the author: 'not by the conversion of the godhead into manhood, but by taking of the manhood into God.' He remains not simply the logical subject of this proposition: 'He was incarnate'; but ontologically he is the author of the act: in the sense of act in which this incarnating may be spoken of as such. But what of this act?

It is the establishment of a new relation between humanity and God, one that is absolutely new. But what is humanity here? Do we speak of that which is particular or of that which is universal? Do we wish to say that God establishes a new relation to the human individual Jesus of Nazareth such as he has had with none other before or after? Are we saying that this absolutely originating creativity is shown in a kind of thrusting of this actual Jesus into relation with himself of an absolutely unprecedented sort? Or are we saying more? What does this verb *establish* mean here? Does it presuppose two finished terms that are to be brought into relation one with another? Or is it claiming that where the *humanum* of Jesus is concerned, it is created as if demanding the divine as its *suppositum*, as if all the while finding itself for what it is in that relation: yet not so as to suggest that that to which it is related is itself a craving of this relation. And if it says the latter, what of that divine term? Is it effected by being thus the *suppositum*, the ὑποκείμενον, of a *humanum* humanly complete; or is it in external relation as to that which is peripherally accidental to it? Even to treat the humanity of Jesus as the *qualitas* of the divine *suppositum* would be to come perilously close to a monophysite view, diminishing the status of that which the Word assumes to a qualification of its unchangeable essence.

Yet thus to plunge into ontological analysis is to risk

173

substituting for the beckoning, questioning concreteness of the life of Jesus a 'ballet-dance of bloodless abstractions', in whose sophisticated gyrations the most precious heart of the mystery is abandoned, or lost sight of. Therefore we do well to return to scrutinize the sense in which the Incarnation may be spoken of as an act. Continually in this discussion, familiar or relatively familiar terms are bent to novel employment. For the Incarnation, if we may characterize it as an act, is not an act in the sense in which Christ's preaching of non-resistance, his healings, his entry into Jerusalem, his dramatic intervention in the temple-courts are isolatable, locatable, datable, acts belonging to the same century as Tiberius' retirement to Capreae, the murder of Caligula, the conspiracy of Messalina against her husband, the sack of Jerusalem by Titus and its sequelae. For the act of the Incarnation is the provision, the positing, and the sustaining of the context within which the individual items of Christ's biography, whether known or irrevocably lost, fall. But what is the 'positing and sustaining of a context'? What indeed is a context in this connection? Does the invocation of the notion here throw any greater light than that of *suppositum*? The phrase 'positing the context' suggests the provision of a setting, almost the over-all direction of a play, in which, as in many human biographies, there is a strange oscillation between that which is unexpected and almost random, and that which can be seen as contributing to an immanent design. Yet for the doctrine of the Incarnation, the context of the experiences is established through their being properly regarded as the experiences of the Son of God who is their subject. It is their ascription to the Eternal as the One whose experiences ultimately they are: this though they are also the experiences of the man Jesus of Nazareth, the experiences which go to render him what he is. When we speak of the experiences as at one and the same time the experiences of this man, this historical individual, and of the Eternal, what are we saying? How are we indeed in this question using the phrase 'at one and the same time'? Yet it may be a little nearer, I will not say, *the* heart, but one depth of our problem: how can that which is necessarily realized in and through a particular point of time, namely a human life, belong to the eternal in such a bondage that we can without exaggeration speak of that life as being the very human life of the Eternal? How can this Eternal have a human life, that which is immutably itself know the succession of a human career? And the questions we advertise by the interrogative *How*? are many and complex. One may say that the concept of the hypostatic union is invoked in the attempt humanly to answer the question: How shall these things be? Yet is it such an answer? Is it not rather a sharp affirmation of the problem created by the belief that they are so? Yet even the possibly flimsy, one could say even tawdry image of stage direction and the vaguer, more dignified complement of authorship emphasize that it is the Creator, the one through whom all things came into being, who is uniquely at work here: that in the Incarnation, God draws near to men.

So in crudely mythological idiom, it suggests not only an event in time but a movement in space. In the so-called 'Nicene Creed' the daunting obscurity of the *homoousion* is followed by statement that is even more dauntingly mythological, suggestive indeed of the *deus ex machina*, resonant with the theological emphasis so eloquently trounced by the late Professor C. E. Raven, which treats the created universe as no more than the stage-set for the drama of redemption: 'Who for us men and for our salvation came down from heaven.[4] Certainly we did not need to wait for Rudolf Bultmann to stress the brash, vulgar crudity of the images, or to remind us that such confession is only unforced on the lips of men and women living in a pre-Copernican world. Yet is not such language

---

[4] There is no suggestion here of the distinctive character of *Platonic* myth.

indispensable in that without it the underlying conviction which arguably the Chalcedonian definition seeks clumsily enough to demythologize would go unformulated? In the order of the 'Nicene' confession the *homoousion* precedes the lapse into mythological idiom: the category of substance is invoked to insist that the faith of Trinity and of Incarnation is monotheistic. There indeed lies the deepest problematic of the former, even as it safeguards the latter from degradation into cult of demigod or hero. The conception of the hypostatic union lies, as it were, the other side both of primary ontological and of mythologically formulated confession. It seeks indeed to 'demythologize' the latter: this though claiming enough at first sight for it to seem to swing giddily between subordinating faith to dexterity in the specialist world of abstract ontology (compare Dr P. T. Forsyth's use of the term 'Chalcedonism' as a pejorative) and offering as an exposition *mysterii verbi incarnati* what to schematizing imagination must seem a gimcrack construction: and this as an account of the one who bids men and women come to him to find rest for their souls, who taught and healed, who prayed and suffered. Yet we have perhaps implied enough that such imaginative schematization is an indulgence, and that the subtlety of ontological exploration is forfeit by such wilfulness. Moreover as the order of the statement in the 'Nicene' confession may have suggested, such explanation is not intended to absorb, and render superfluous, the more haunting and appealing idiom of myth, but to complement and discipline it. By our reckoning the Chalcedonian formula assumes a conception of divine transcendence, of what in conscious rejection of a seemingly attractive metaphysical immanentism, Søren Kierkegaard called 'the infinite qualitative difference between God and man'. Yet as Kierkegaard himself emphasized, in many places (never more forcefully perhaps than in the work that should be known as 'Training *into* Christianity'), this transcendent, even if to entertain the possibility of its change was to entertain a self-contradiction, has been bound, or rather has bound itself in inseparable union with the manhood of Jesus of Nazareth.

'Behold the great creator makes himself a house of clay: a robe of virgin flesh he takes, which he will wear for aye.' Or again in the words of Ambrose: 'O equal of the Father Thou, Thy fleshly mantle gird on now.' The metaphors are hackneyed enough, and one is right quickly to point out that a man or woman may lay that coat, that scarf, that mantle aside when they come indoors from the cold. The carol carefully insists that the robe of human flesh (and here flesh must be understood as flesh and blood: human nature) is taken 'for aye', emphatically not to be discarded as one suit of clothes may be laid aside and replaced by another. Yet in it too the image is invoked to bring out the sheer externality of relation between godhead and manhood. If the latter only exists in the former (whatever precisely 'in' may there indicate), there is no infusion (a misleading word, but employed to suggest) of godhead into manhood: no effective communication of the very substance (*deutera ousia*) of former to latter. The *communicatio idiomatum* is construed as hardly more than a licence to carry out certain linguistic substitutions in speaking, for instance, of Jesus' weariness, and God's power in him. So by arbitrary, supposedly divine permission it may speak of God as weary and the dying Jesus as omnipotent: 'Quaerens me sedisti lassus; Redemisti crucem passus'. But the exhaustion was the Nazarene's, the agonized endurance his: yet because of this mystery of union, it can kindle our devotion by speaking of them as God's own. Hardly more than a linguistic licence? Yes: a little more, for the arbitrariness of the conventional permission is grounded in incommensurable fact. One might perhaps say that as well as permissible, notional indulgence it is proper acclamation. But *what* is being acclaimed?

Yet an effort was made (as was noticed above) to present the manhood of the concrete identifiable man, Jesus of Nazareth, as radically affected by its assumption by the Eternal. So it is insisted that he becomes not *a* man, but manhood. God the Son is the ultimate subject of the act of assumption, and manhood assumed by God forfeits, through that assumption, its identifiable particularity: this though, of course, it is never intended that Jesus of Nazareth ceases to be distinguishable as an individual from his contemporaries. 'Whom seek ye?' 'Jesus of Nazareth.' Rather what is intended is that that altogether unique relation to the Eternal that we name hypostatic union is *malgré tout* internal to the term assumed in such a way that it is constituted by an openness to the divine so uniquely thoroughgoing (I had almost said absolutely) that it is rendered in itself impersonal. Any corresponding reciprocity between godhead and manhood is denied as ultimately imperilling the sovereign freedom of the Divine, expressed in the redemption of the human race, and its very changelessness.

So we seem to have moved back as it were in a circle, to the previous point of concentration on the *act of assumption*: this seemingly impenetrable mystery constitutive of the Incarnate Word. Of course the modern student is and must be appalled by the subordination of the searching simplicities of the synoptic Gospels, even their peculiar strangeness, to this obsessive preoccupation with twisted ontological categories. We are all Antiochenes rather than Alexandrines now: and to many it must seem as if the approach of this study deprives it instantly of claim to serious attention in that for the most part it *seems* to proceed 'from above downwards' and not 'from below upwards'. Disputes concerning theological method are, however, often tedious and time-wasting: there is a very great deal to be said for the maxim: 'Tackle the problem and the methodological principles will take care of themselves.' But at this point it is perhaps permissible, possibly even necessary, to insert a reference to this frequently parroted antithesis.

Of course the language in which the opposition is expressed is metaphorical: 'from below upwards': 'from above downwards'. What we are concerned with is God and man. Do we in positing the Incarnation move from God to man or from man to God? To some the answer might be thought obvious in as much as we are men and women. Yet is it quite like this? For Christ comes before us, or at least it is possible that he is in fact so presented, as one who violates the contrast, or in old-fashioned evangelical language, bridges or straddles the gulf between human and divine: and this he does not by arrogance of assertive claim, but by a strange, haunting alternation, even interpenetration of humility and authority, receptivity and confident demand. So in a profoundly suggestive phrase, the late Dr. W. R. Inge spoke of 'an infinite self-abnegation' as the characteristic hallmark of the fourth Evangelist's portrait of the Son of God. If we are interrogated by Christ across the centuries: 'Who do you say that I am?', in our answer it is our conceptions at once of the actuality of divine existence and of the possibilities of human that are brought to the bar of a questioning more devastating, more searching, and (must we not say?) more intellectually demanding than the Socratic. We are made to be drawn in all directions at once, and where the emphasis of this study is concerned, to engage at once with time and eternity, with temporal and eternal.

Certainly to write in these terms is to commit oneself to a particular view or to one of a number of particular views concerning the New Testament documents, in particular concerning the status of the portraits of the central figure. One need not claim for these portraits (and the use of the plural is deliberate) the verisimilitude of a set of Identikit pictures or passport photographs, or indeed the kind of accuracy found, for instance, in John Grigg's major biography of Lloyd George or for that matter claim for them as much as may be claimed for Plutarch's lives of Pericles and Pompey, Aristides and Brutus.

One should not attempt to iron out the inconsistencies, but rather to see their presence as an invitation to more searching enquiry: finding in that presence evidence that the reality of Jesus defied any sort of easy, and indeed most sorts of comparatively painful, assimilation. This strangeness may be judged rooted in, and expressive of, the way in which he lived uniquely as the frontier of the familiar and the transcendent, the relative and the absolute, and by so standing, demands that our every conception of both alike be revised.

Where the traditional theologies of the Incarnation may be thought to have gone astray lies in a surrender to an uncriticized, even deeply mistaken conception of divine transcendence. One might say that while their grasp of the unique denotation of the term 'transcendent' was obstinately correct, their refusal to allow its uniqueness of reference to be queried, or the incommensurability of divine and human to be challenged absolutely justified, yet there was a failure to allow that divine sovereignty might contain within itself the foundation of divine self-limitation. Or more precisely there was a failure to ask how far the Trinitarian conception of God as he is in himself (the doctrine of an essential as distinct from an economic Trinity) compelled transformation of the understanding of transcendence?

The connotation of the term 'transcendent' was found too easily in terms of an absolutely immutable self-sufficiency, an invulnerable aseity, formally defensible but certainly demanding reconstruction in the light of Christian reality. The mistake involved in insisting that while the world is related to God in a dependence to which that of a song or the singer who is singing it is a remote, but not wholly ineffective analogy, to speak of him as related to the world in any other than a purely notional sense is a radical mistake. It is a mistake because while seeking to safeguard what may be characterized mythologically as divine immunity from involvement in the affairs of the world, securing an infinite, unaffected resourcefulness in creative design, it achieves such a safeguard only at the cost of rendering the exercise of such resource virtually self-contradictory. It is as if to secure the possibility of the radically self-initiated, one rendered impossible its execution. And it is in the actuality as distinct from any sort of abstract possibility of such execution that the *point de départ* of Christian confession is found: that is in Jesus of Nazareth in whom the incommensurables of God and man are found united, or in whom, and by whom the problem of the 'flow' of their union is raised by the daunting dizzying presence of its reality.

What light can be thrown on our central problem if it engages more closely now with the theme of temporal and eternal, with the manner of their relation in Jesus? And here a word of warning lest such procedure seem to be a necessarily futile quasi-biographical essay seeking to trace the 'development of Christ's messianic consciousness'. While nothing is gained by the attempt to reconstruct empathetically the supposed gradually maturing self-identification of Jesus with the deutero-Isaianic 'servant', it is equally a mistake to avert attention from the deeply significant spatial and temporal armature of the Gospel narrative. The importance in the synoptic presentation of the movement from Galilee to Jerusalem is familiar enough; but equally significant is the continued reference to an hour that is not yet come to one known only to the Father, to one that might pass, to one that is come. There is a time as well as a place for the death of a prophet. Further, in the Fourth Gospel this movement from one place to another, this waiting for that which is not yet come, and acclaiming the same when it is come, is set in the context of a mission from the Father into the world and back to the Father: a mission that contains within its design its initiation, its execution, and its end, its settings, its occasions, and its final issue. The word *mission* is, as we shall see, of crucial importance.

It is not only, as Professor Christopher Evans has pointed out, that *ho pempsas me Patēr* is for the fourth evangelist a deeply pregnant designation of God himself; it is also as Hans Urs von Balthasar has profoundly argued in *Theodramatik*[5] ii.2) that *mission* is a christological category of very powerful import inasmuch as the *missiones ad extra personarum unius individuae Trinitatis* are grounded in and expressions of the processional interior life of God.

There is suggested by the New Testament documents, and in particular the Fourth Gospel an ontology of the relations of eternity to time, constructed or reconstructed in the light of the focusing of those relations in Jesus. It may be that one of the most important intellectual shifts accomplished in New Testament theology is the movement from an eschatology on occasion flamboyantly apocalyptic in its imagery to a Christological concentration, always theocentric, but insisting that some of the riddles tradition had bequeathed as unsolved problems should be translated into terms of relationships realized in a human career, lying indeed at its very foundation.

Where the Gospels pass from the quasi-biographical to the overtly theological is the place at which this issue is allowed to arise, and not only to arise, but to focus an always questioning faith on the figure of a man: as if here is the point at which faith must seek to mature itself by the effort of understanding. The problem of Christology arises most acutely when it occurs almost as the inhumanization of the issue of the relation of the temporal to the eternal, the transformation of that issue into the one of the ontological structure of Christ's person, the interpenetration of these incommensurables in the unfathomably mysterious texture of his being: at once God and man.

[5] Einsiedeln, 1978. See my essay in the volume *The Analogy of Beauty*, edited by John Riches (T. & T. Clark, 1986).

But if faith must seek understanding, in its quest it joins understanding seeking faith. A proper theology must always allow the point of junction to be crucial. Furthermore it has been indicated that the doctrine of the Incarnation assumes *a* doctrine of creation. The use of the indefinite article, not *the* but *a* doctrine of creation, is quite intentional; for if formally the thesis that God is creator of all things visible and invisible remains identical across the centuries, it would be obscurantist folly to ignore as of only secondary significance our enlarged understanding both of the scale and detail of the creative process. Yet this understanding which we are right to recognize as something to be won rather than as assured possession is assumed in the elaboration of the doctrine of the Incarnation. For the One of whom we predicate Incarnation is the One through whom the foundations of the universe have been laid and sustained, and it is through insisting that in Jesus of Nazareth He is uniquely present that we attribute (in a synthetic proposition) divinity to him. But what of the manner of this presence? Enough has been said to show how important for enlarging our insight into the meaning of this presence is sensitivity to the range of issues comprised under the rubric— the relation of time to eternity. And time, whether or not we agree with Augustine in his insistence that time came into being with creation, is the most pervasive structural form of the world as we know it.

If however we allow the mystery of the Incarnation to shed its light upon the formal order of relations of creature to creator, and creator to creature, and if we give to that mystery the authority it claims, we must reverse any understanding of divine transcendence that sees transcendence as only safeguarded by refusal to admit any sort of self-limitation into the divine, any sort of self-committal in creation that would allow a genuine, if assymmetrical, reciprocity in relations of creation and creator. Of course God must (and the *must* is of logical necessity) remain invulnerable. One might say that his aseity can be mythologized in terms of an ultimate invulnerability.[6]

Such idioms of course allow the indulgence of representing God as in time; for it is through time that what is at risk is procured. 'And thou continuest holy, O thou worship of Israel' (Ps. 22).[7] Yet if it is an invulnerability that is acclaimed here, it is not one of indifference: but urged with a thrust that is of love as well as of dignity. But it must not suggest a conflict, as if there were temptation as most certainly was met by Jesus. The threat to the being of the Incarnate which is suggested by the tradition of the forty days' ordeal in the desert (recapitulation of the experience of the children of Israel, but very much more than that) is as it were projection, a resonance in time and space, of that which in fact is the unfathomable actuality of his presence to, and not just over against, the world he has brought into being, is sustaining, is bringing to fulfilment. In human terms such presence is affirmed in terms of a victory over sceptical despair: but *in se*, what is it—this presence of the threefold God to his world? If we must excise from the concept we form of it any hint of conflict, of struggle, even of the peace that is achieved through such engagement, how are we to convey to ourselves that energy, that unceasingly urgent concern which belongs of necessity to its actuality? Again we must plunge into abstraction: but what sort of abstraction? Surely a very special sort that seeks to capture in its elemental purity the texture of the divine creative presence.

There is another question that must however be advanced here, and that is the involvement of God in his threefold being in the Incarnation. We shall find it possible to suggest in a pioneering essay in utterance of the unutterable that the very unity of the threefold God is as it were put at risk in the Incarnation, in

[6] But see Epilogue for further reflection on this invulnerability.
[7] Ps. 22.—B.C.P. version.

184

Jesus' total dependence on faith and prayer in his temptation. (The point may be illustrated by the initial Western misgivings over the formula 'one of the Trinity became incarnate', proposed by the Scythian monks at Rome in 519, and successfully advocated by implication in Boethius' *opuscula*.) 'O wisest love! that flesh and blood, which did in Adam fail, should strive afresh against their foe, should strive and should prevail.' 'And that a higher gift than grace, should flesh and blood refine: God's presence and his very self and essence all divine.' And this refinement is won through that 'very self and essence all divine' putting itself (*in essentia unitas, in personis proprietas, in maiestate aequalitas*) at risk through demanding its affirmation, its sustained defence, in conditions of human ordeal. Can we speak in sense reaching beyond nominal *communicatio idiomatum* of a divine ordeal? If we do so, it is in the setting of the hypostatic union as it were, bringing to unforeseeable, spontaneous completion in unimaginable fullness of self-communication that to which in principle at least a tentative commitment has been made in creation, is indeed made all the while. One can by no logical sleight of hand conjure the ultimate intimacy of divine self-exposure out of the relation of creator to creation. Yet creation provides the parables through which we can represent to ourselves the impending mystery.

Again: a word on method. The heart of the problem facing anyone who essays a treatise *de verbo Incarnato* is the oscillation, the alternation of *language* that is abstractly ontological with language that is mythological, crudely anthropomorphic. In part the former provides the means of disciplining the latter, or rendering its use aseptic, proof against the corruption of the imagination. But there is more to it than that: for the anthropomorphic is as it were penetrated by the ontological styles, bent and twisted till the very concept of God as he is in himself is suffused by its emphases. It is as if a new piety was born, a piety that imagination can find in the Gospels. But it is

185

with time and eternity that we are first and foremost concerned, and it is to this relation that we must now turn: to time and eternity, but also to space and omnipresence.

'Of that hour knoweth no man, not the angels in heaven nor the Son but the Father only.' This logion is a clear statement that for the Son in his Incarnate existence, as the one whose very being consists in his-being-sent, the ultimate secrets are to be received: not immediately transparent, but painfully won. There is no transcendence of the pervasive temporal, no leaping over its condition. What constitutes such limitation *in arcanis aeternae deitatis* we cannot know: receptivity as a moment in absolute being is something to be affirmed as mystery. But it is the ground of that which we encounter in the temporal experience of Jesus. And his experience is most certainly temporal in form.

'Jesus increased in wisdom and stature, and in favour with God and man.' It is at the age of 12 that he is taken by his parents to Jerusalem for Passover, when he reminds them that on this very advance into maturity, he must be about his Father's affairs in his Father's house, that temple which is so crucial a locale in the Lucan writings. Time, place, movement: these pervasive forms of human experience are the forms of the experience of Jesus. Even if we must agree that the order of Jesus' history, as we have received it, is imposed on the events that make it up by the evangelists, so that in fact we cannot confidently speak of *the* order in which the events happened (and I am not thinking simply of the differences between Synoptic and Johannine schematizations), yet still the writers are concerned with what is in itself a temporal series in which there was an actual before and after. And this before and after was something received, and something fashioned out of what was received. There was, for instance, a 'not yet'; 'my hour is not yet come'. Yet that hour was not something passively awaited: 'Sleep on now, and take your rest: the hour is come: the Son of Man is betrayed.' It is not mere catastrophe, but an action that Jesus goes forth to meet. And this because it is his Father's will, and the hour something he receives from the Father's hand. The delicacy of interplay is discernible across the construction of the writers who are responding to the temporality of Jesus' experience by the shape of their representation. So their memories (and I should try to clarify my use of the term here) constitute essays in the recapture of his self-consciousness as that was fashioned through response to the world ordered by him, as that world impinged on him. An old-fashioned exegesis sought to trace 'the development of the Messianic consciousness' of Jesus, treating, for instance, his baptism in the Jordan as a crucial episode in the advance of his self-identification with the Christ. But to limit his self-identification to such a moment is to ignore the extent to which it was achieved through a multitude of relations, through receptivity and response. There is a sense in which the value he gives to the variable. 'There is an x, such that I am x and no one is x who is not identified with myself' remains open; it is always for his Father to assign that value, and its assignation is clearly bound up with the identification of his hour. What is his hour? What the hour of the Son of Man? What that of the power of darkness? And this hour is crucial in a human life; how is it related to the eternal? And how both alike to the raising of the Son from the dead? That has a date; it has its before and after. Yet it is also the eternization of the life of the Son; this in the sense of giving it a universal contemporaneity, but not in such a way that nothing happened in the raising which was not in itself unique, and which is reflected in that which is contemporaneous.

'Christ being raised from the dead dieth no more; death has no more dominion over him.' We may indeed by an effort of imaginative abstraction force ourselves to attend to the detailed particularity of the Incarnate life, deliberately stripping what we imagine to ourselves bare of the least hint of the perceptibly numinous; indeed such representation is necessary to convey to ourselves the thrust of the kenosis. But what is contemporary is that which through his Father's act in raising him Christ has become. What does it imply for our understanding of time that in time there has been accomplished not simply the eternization of a particular biography but the constitution of that biography as the way for the insertion of all human circumstance into the tapestry of the eternal? And how is this insertion related to the presence of the eternal in the details of that history, to the return of the eternal so present, to the role of that eternal in the constitution of the time-order?

Chapter 12

PIERRE TEILHARD DE CHARDIN'S
LE MILIEU DIVIN

The work entitled *Le Milieu Divin*, characterized by the author as 'an essay on the interior life', was written at Tientsin between November 1926 and March 1927. The French editor adds a note on the last page, in which he quotes from a final profession of faith made by Père Teilhard de Chardin in March 1955, the last month of his life, in which he emphasizes the fact that this short book, together with his haunting essay *La Messe sur le Monde*, contains his fundamental vision. The censorship to which his writings were subject prevented its publication in French till 1957; three years later Collins published an English translation. It should be said at the outset of any revised assessment that all who can, should read this book in the original French. The translators did their best; but they were totally unable to convey the texture and subtlety of the author's French prose. This, though inevitable, is in every way a pity as no other of his works (except various papers), is more successful in distilling his essential vision, and enabling the reader to appreciate for himself its importance.

Further, it is significant that in a work which the author regards as an essay on the interior life, his thought achieves a disciplined clarity that it quite frequently loses in later writings, where a kind of sentimental evolutionary optimism is allowed to blur the realities of twentieth century existence. Of course Teilhard was always an optimist. But the reader of *Le Milieu Divin* is often reminded that its author is the fellow-countryman of Descartes and Pascal. To mention the latter name in particular may seem absurd; but in this prolonged colloquy with himself and with his God, Teilhard returns again and again to the place of human existence in a universe whose dimensions, both spatial and temporal, defy the reach of imagination. If the discontinuities of Pascal's 'three realms' are profoundly alien to him, he remains convinced of the dignity of his priesthood as something unique. If at times the reader is reminded of the philistine crudity of the scholastic theology Teilhard and his contemporaries (who included a number of men of outstanding promise), learnt in the theologate of the Society of Jesus after *Pascendi*, he is also made aware of the depth of his spiritual training.

Teilhard was incapable of writing a formal theological treatise on the doctrine of the Incarnation. Yet if on page 136 he reveals himself as honestly perplexed by 'the disconcerting multiplicity of individuals', in the same section of his book he affirms a passionate Christo-centrism. I say 'affirms', because this profession belongs to a work of meditation, rather than of formal theology. This though the reader has to work hard if he is to make its teaching his own, and *most important*, if he is to improve on Teilhard by a sharper grasp of the discontinuities the writer is enabled by his vision to brush aside too lightly.

It was unfortunate that Teilhard was so continually deprived of the kind of association he needed with his equals, working in other areas and out of different intellectual experience in the Society of Jesus. On pages 73 and 74 the French editor gives a summary of Teilhard's spiritual doctrine which he set out in a letter to Père Auguste Valensin, one of his closest friends in the Society of Jesus, and a man of undoubted achievement as a philosopher, capable, for instance, of summarizing with masterly insight aspects of Kant's theory of knowledge within the confines of an encyclopaedia article.[1] This letter shows the sort of intellectually disciplined presentation that Teilhard could

[1] My attention was called to Valensin's article on Kant many years before I even knew of Teilhard's existence!

offer of his ideas, when constrained to present them to a man of Valensin's calibre. In these paragraphs he is, in fact, summarizing his ascetic theology, indicating the way in which a man may school himself to reconcile in his life acceptance of the universe in its astonishing and utterly fascinating complexity with the sort of self-abnegation that the ever-present fact of death (if nothing else), reveals as inevitably our human lot.

On page 131, in most striking language, Teilhard insists that:

> God does not offer Himself to our finite beings as a thing all complete and ready to be embraced. For us He is eternal discovery and eternal growth. The more we think we understand Him, the more He reveals Himself as otherwise.

By itself this quotation might suggest that Teilhard's God was akin to that suggested in the metaphysical writings of Samuel Alexander and A. N. Whitehead, for both of whom, in different ways, God is coming to be with the development of the universe; His achievement lies in the future, as much for himself as for His universe. But to understand Teilhard's language in this way would be to ignore the title of the book, which very wisely those responsible for its translation decided to retain. The universe is the *milieu*, sustained by its creator, pervaded by his continuing presence, in its minutest detail the object of his concern and the place of his possible self-disclosure to men and women. In an article written in the early sixties,[2] his fellow Jesuit, the late Cardinal Jean Daniélou, remarked that Teilhard had devastatingly criticized the very widespread conception of God as a *deus ex machina*, intervening to correct what had gone awry, or at least sometimes doing so, but grandly indifferent to the whole process of his world. It was indeed this aspect of his work that helped to make the late

[2] *Études*, 1961.

Professor C. E. Raven so devoted an advocate of Teilhard's ideas in the last years of his life. He found in his writing a marvellous corrective of the theological habit of treating the natural universe as the mere stage-setting for the drama of redemption. In their different ways Daniélou and Raven seem to me to bring out the essential lessons still to be learnt from this book, but only by the reader who is prepared to give time to its study.

Teilhard writes in the first instance to correct the philistine narrowness of vision, the gross deficiency of spiritual imagination, that he finds among the devout in their attitudes to the universe, and also to the majesty of the human mind's achievement in penetrating its secrets. He emphasizes indeed that this penetration is only in its relatively early stages, and he is aware, without indulgence in the unbalanced technological optimism of his later writings, that the growth in understanding will be fulfilled in a transformation of our whole environment. He would indeed baptize the image of Prometheus. But if Prometheus is to measure up to the reality of his humanity, he must recall that in human life, moving as it does from the cradle to the grave, there is an inescapable place for passivity (Teilhard's own word), as well as for the activity that he stresses, glorying in the affirmation of its spiritual significance. It is perhaps a pity that he was not helped by his friend Valensin to formulate in this work the epistemological import of this duality which he so rightly stresses in its pages.

The book was written nearly sixty years ago, and the English translation has now been available for 26 years. Hitherto I have been concerned to treat of its general significance, leaving indeed unmentioned its acknowledged weakness (of which the writer shows himself more than a little aware), in treatment of sin and evil. This omission was deliberate; for it seemed best to treat of this issue in assessing the impact of the book of the contemporary reader. Although the work is innocent of the culpably facile optimism which marred many of Teilhard's later essays, it remains necessary for the reader to ask himself precisely what the lessons were which Teilhard had learnt from his experience on the Western Front in the first world war, articulated with unsparing honesty in his correspondence. These letters assure the reader of the writer's courage; but they also raise inescapable questions concerning the moral quality of his political vision.

Where the contemporary reader has lessons to learn from this book, particularly relevant to his situation, is in the style of its bold and often *unexpected* christo-centrism. The reader who comes to the pages in which the author affirms the centrality of the life and work of Christ for the whole universe, from a knowledge of recent Christological writing, will undoubtedly be shocked by the passionate confidence in which he makes this confession of faith. He is not writing apologetics, but inviting the reader to follow him in an exercise of imagination and spiritual perception, through which he may so enlarge his sense of the mission of the Crucified that it encompasses the world which is still very much coming to be, and at the same time bring that world within the terms of that historical episode, as if there to find its foundation and its secret. So he writes on page 105:

If you suppress the historical reality of Christ, the divine omnipresence which intoxicates us becomes, like all the other dreams of metaphysics, uncertain, vague, conventional— lacking the decisive experimental verification by which to impose itself on our minds, and without the moral authority to assimilate our lives into it.

The pages in the book which treat of such topics as the person of Christ, the Eucharist, and the *parousia* are curiously fragmentary, scattered about the centre of the work, providing no easy road to their understanding, except that offered by the whole essay. Yet the pages treating of Christ and his cross must still shake the modern reader by their bold avoidance of any taint of religious, let alone sectarian, provincialism. And this from a writer who quotes with admiration a characteristic short story by Robert Hugh Benson! It is as if the way these pages raise the question of the relation to Christ to the universe is still significant as a corrective of forms of theological parochialism as powerful as those against which in their different ways both Teilhard and Raven revolted.

The religious parochialism I have in mind is subtly different, focussed perhaps by the controversy around the volume: *The Myth of God Incarnate*. This in spite of the essayists' desire to liberate Christian theology from an indifference to the spiritual resources of other religious traditions. The cosmological dimension in which Teilhard's experience as a palaeontologist constrained his imagination to roam is still neglected, and that in a period in which, more even than during his life-time, we should be straining radically to enlarge and correct our perspectives, for instance in relation to time and space. To read this book today should move the reader to see the need not to rehearse its ideas, but to attempt a comparable study in which the question of the cosmological significance of Christ's life and work (rightly a perennial theme of Christian speculation since Paul's letter to the Romans) may be envisaged anew. Perhaps such essays must always have about them something of the character of Kant's 'Ideas of Reason', speculative ideals that we must continually seek to reach, but which we must accept that we can never completely achieve.[3] Yet without the imperative to attempt them, Christian experience must be gravely impoverished. If Whitehead is right in speaking of Christianity

---

[3] Kant contrasted the role of these 'Ideas' in human knowledge as 'regulative' with that of the categories as 'constitutive', (or sheerly indispensable).

as a religion perennially in search of a metaphysic, but never able to rest in one, we must also say that faith must ever seek to fulfil itself in vision, yet know that its quest must always ultimately fail, and require to be begun anew.

But one further word must be added. Anyone seeking to re-write this book for the world in which we live, would have to remember that where theology and especially the sort of theologically disciplined spirituality that Teilhard is writing are concerned, any essay must be condemned as ultimately frivolous, which does not reckon with the reality of Auschwitz. If we need more than ever the kind of guidance such books as Teilhard's may give us in enlarging our perspectives, we have to assure ourselves that at the same time we do not forget that the age in which we live is that which has seen the Holocaust, and is marked indelibly by its consequences. If we certainly need to ponder anew in 1986 the lessons that this short book has still to teach us, we must also re-fashion at a more tragic personal depth, our understanding of redemption. For if Teilhard is right in supposing the future of the universe to be in our own hands, we must not forget that those hands are stained indelibly and that Prometheus has proved himself repeatedly, and may prove himself irreversibly again in the future, author of his world's destruction, rather than promoter of its growth.

Chapter 13

CRUCIFIXION—RESURRECTION

Crucifixion—Resurrection. The Pattern of the Theology and Ethics of the New Testament.
Edwyn Clement Hoskyns, Bart., DD, and Francis Noel Davey. Edited with a biographical introduction by Gordon S. Wakefield. London S.P.C.K., 1981. £18.00, pp. XVI and 384.

In the spring of 1937 a book was advertised as forthcoming from Faber, entitled *Crucifixion—Resurrection* by Sir Edwyn Clement Hoskyns and Noel Davey. But in the afternoon of Monday, 28th June 1937, six weeks short of his 53rd birthday, Sir Edwyn Hoskyns died. The work was in fact unfinished, and although Dr Davey hoped to bring it out, he felt bound to give precedence to Hoskyns' other unfinished work, his commentary on the Fourth Gospel, which Faber published in February 1940. A litle more than two years later, Davey failed to secure renewal of his University post in Cambridge, and returned to parish work at Coddenham in Suffolk. In January 1945 he succeeded Dr W. K. Lowther Clarke as editorial secretary of the S.P.C.K.; he had, in fact, moved to London to work with Dr Clarke six months earlier, before taking over from him. In this work he continued till the end of 1970, fully intending in his retirement to complete the work on which he had embarked with Hoskyns in the middle thirties. But he had hardly begun this task when he died, leaving material of his own which is included in the book which Gordon Wakefield has now produced.

It is impossible to praise the editorial work that Dr Wakefield has done highly enough. He has succeeded in presenting the *disjecta membra* of the work on which Hoskyns and Davey had embarked, in a way that makes of their whole undertaking something coherent and intelligible, supplementing the unfinished material of the book with later work from Davey's own hand. He has added a sermon which apparently Hoskyns gave in Wigan Parish Church on Easter Day 1933, and which Davey repeated in Cambridge on Easter Day 1972, not long before he himself died, and has rounded off the volume with an editorial epilogue, combining perception and restraint. He has also prefaced his presentation of the unfinished book with a short memoir of Dr Davey, and a much longer biographical study of Sir Edwyn Hoskyns. Between the two he has inserted the very remarkable University sermon which Davey gave on 8th March 1942, a very few hours after he had heard of his mother's death. If, as he *suggests*, its manner was used in evidence against Davey when later in the year the question of the renewal of his Cambridge lectureship came up, its invocation in that connection is a sad judgement on the discrimination of those concerned with that appointment in the Cambridge faculty: (I write here as myself a professorial member of that faculty from 1960 to 1978.) To the matter contained in this sermon I shall turn later.

The memoir of Sir Edwyn Hoskyns is very well done. In fifty-four pages (pp. 27–81) Wakefield succeeds in presenting his subject 'warts and all'; but while he does not shrink from, e.g. the issues raised acutely by Hoskyns' association with Dr Gerhard Kittel,[A] and by the latter's notorious anti-semitism, he also succeeds by the extracts from Hoskyns' writings which he quotes, in showing the insight of which he was frequently capable. If it is a mark of genuine achievement in theology or philosophy for a man or woman to enable his own judgement to be corrected from his own writings, Wakefield succeeds in showing that to be true of Hoskyns. It was, of course, Corpus Christi College, Cambridge, that gave the young Hoskyns his opportunity. In particular, it was Will Spens, whose book *Belief and Practice* Hoskyns read on its publication in 1917 while serving as a chaplain in France, who insisted that the College elected the young man into a fellowship, which he was to take up at the end of the War. Spens believed that he saw in Hoskyns one who would expound, with particular reference to the scriptures of the New Testament, the sort of 'catholic modernism' that he had himself outlined in his book, and on his return to Cambridge (where he had studied as an undergraduate), this was, in fact, what Hoskyns began by doing. At the same time he accepted the political and social Toryism with which by then, the College was becoming identified, following here the inspiration of one of its most influential Fellows, Geoffrey Butler, whose book *The Tory Tradition* still deserves the attention of students of political theory. There is no doubt that the young Hoskyns (in spite of his experiences as a curate in Sunderland, and then as a chaplain in the First World War), found these attitudes congenial; indeed Wakefield is honest enough to include the burden of the slightly ridiculous College office of President among the much more serious tasks which weighed on him in the last year of his life. But if Hoskyns yielded too easily to the pressure on him of College assumption and habit, in theology he quickly found his own way. Wakefield does not probe in detail his relations with Will Spens; but on page 71 he includes Hoskyns' devastating judgement on the latter's peculiar religious attitudes. It was in 1933, when he was nearly 50, that Hoskyns published with the Oxford University Press, his translation of Karl Barth's commentary on the Epistle to the Romans. Inevitably the labour which he spent on this work led to his being called a Barthian; indeed the label had been attached to him already. But when one recalls that translation in the light of sermons of the same period published posthumously, in the light of the commentary on the Fourth Gospel, and still more in the light of *Crucifixion—Resurrection*, one sees that what Hoskyns learnt

198

from Barth enabled him present, as very few of his generation, the epistemological problems lying at the heart of Christian belief.

It may seem a paradox to pay such a tribute to one who was not in any sense a philosopher. Yet from more than 40 years distance the present reviewer recalls that it was Hoskyns' commentary on the Fourth Gospel that enabled him to see that that book in the New Testament canon, raised in the most acute form the central issues touching the relations of faith and sense/perception. It may well be said that the same issues are raised in Bultmann's later great commentary; but that is a tribute to Hoskyns' insight rather than a depreciation of his achievement. What *Crucifixion—Resurrection* adds (and here I include with it Davey's University sermon of 8 March 1942), is a deeper understanding of the underlying theological views on which these epistemological insights rest, and to which, indeed, they point. There are, as we shall see, great tensions involved here, and it is significant that one of the weakest sections in the book (as Wakefield seems to recognize), is that dealing with the Resurrection narratives (pp. 279–292). Indeed, here there is ambiguity of a kind far less discernible in Davey's sermon. Odd though it may seem, some of this weakness could have been avoided through a more explicit recognition of philosophical problems. I say problems advisedly; for in the late Professor O. C. Quick's searching criticism of parts of Hoskyns' work,[1] it is the latter's insensitivity to the wider perceptions opened by philosophy that Quick is reproaching, not (for Quick does not notice this), his failure to take *explicit* notice of the critical

---

[1] Quick's criticism of Hoskyns is to be found in *The Gospel of Divine Action* (Nisbet, 1933). It was developed in lectures, given at Oxford in 1941 and 1942, which sadly have never been published. He failed however to recognize the depth of Hoskyns' epistemological insight, partly because this was an area of philosophy to which he came late in his life; his criticisms were more aimed at Hoskyns' insistence on the unity of the New Testament witness, and his seeming indifference to the gulf between Pauline and Johannine theology.

problems raised by Kant's philosophy[2] and indeed by that of Ludwig Wittgenstein in Hoskyns' own Cambridge. Had he done so, his exploration of the nature of faith would surely have been deepened.

Inevitably the work, both by Hoskyns and Davey, which Wakefield presents, is uneven. There are sections that remain curiously disappointing. Thus the passage (pp. 217–239) entitled: *Father and Son—the Dereliction of Jesus* is half-hearted and incomplete, and the sermon on the Resurrection faith repeated by Davey in Cambridge in 1972, on the last Easter of his life, from a sermon which Hoskyns himself had given in Wigan in 1933, and characterized by the former (p. XV), as a 'simple whoop of triumph', is a pretentious *fervorino* unworthy alike of subject and preacher. On the other hand, Davey's controversial University Sermon of 8th March 1942, is of a very different order; it is remarkable in the depth of its theological understanding, and to dismiss it as an essay in biblical positivism is to be guilty of a serious myopia. Unlike the section on 'Father and Son', it raises explicitly the Trinitarian dimension of Christian theology, inviting a continuing advance towards its completion from such work as Hans Urs von Balthasar's *Theologie der drei Tage*. Indeed one might say that had Davey continued elsewhere the ideas adumbrated in this admittedly very demanding sermon, along the lines of von Balthasar's monograph, he might have eliminated some of the ambiguities discernible in the haunting chapter on the Resurrection narratives (pp. 279–193).

But the greatness of the best sections of this work remains. The ninety pages. (pp. 85–175) that introduce *Crucifixion—Resurrection* are unforgettably impressive. The quotation from Sir George Adam-Smith's *Historical Geography of the Holy Land*

---

[2] Barth in the *Römerbrief* shows considerable familiarity with Kant's Dialectic.

(p. 94) introduced on the previous page by quotation from a personal letter, provides a most striking *mise-en-scène* for presentation of the authors' central theme of the interpenetration of Crucifixion and Resurrection; the omission of the conjunction *and* in the title is very important. The second chapter on the problem of the death of Jesus in the New Testament, which the present reviewer found perhaps the most searching in the whole book, and which he has read many times, shows the deep subtlety of Hoskyns' exegesis, and his capacity for raising the epistemological problems at the very heart of Christian faith. His views are not always easy to grasp, and clearly at times he is attracted to a conception that would treat the Resurrection as, in fact, the means whereby the disciples were enabled to discern the glory of the mutual exchange of Father and Son in the humiliation of Jesus. Yet the 'earthiness' of his theology is continually emphasized. It is revealed, for instance, in his letter from Suez, when as a young chaplain to the Lancashires, he had been deeply stirred by the idealism of a young Socialist, finding in his hopes for the post-war future, what Hoskyns might later have called a parable of authentic eschatology (p. 60). Wakefield is certainly right to note the clear resonance of this relatively affirmative response to the young soldier in a remarkable sermon Hoskyns gave in the chapel of Corpus Christi College in 1933 on the text: Quench not the Spirit. This most impressive address belonged to the time when the influence of his work on the translation of Barth's great commentary on the Epistle to the Romans was strong upon him. But it is also worth noting that it was delivered at a time when he was by no means prepared to condemn outright the grim accompaniments of the Nazi *Machtübernahme*. Yet in this sermon the harshness which undoubtedly marred not a few of his pulpit utterances was markedly lacking, and he showed himself sensitive to the ways in which folly for Christ's sake (typified by the extravagance of the women who anointed him in the house of Simon the Leper) must none the less be seen as 'parables, witnesses, signposts, by which we are led to conceive of the workings and operations of the Holy Spirit of God.' In such addresses as this, Hoskyns revealed that for all the contempt which on occasion marred his judgements on humanitarian optimism, he was at heart humanist.

Certainly in the very important first two chapters of *Crucifixion—Resurrection*, Hoskyns insists that we must reckon, where Christ's coming is concerned, with a radical discontinuity. The reality, and indeed the savage cruelty of his rejection cuts across any facile continuism, which would (as it were) domesticate the bloody scene of the Crucifixion, making it no more than a climactic manifestation of God's beneficence, continuous with the good will shown towards men shown in Jesus' teaching, his acts of power, etc. Hoskyns' presentation of this thesis on pp. 102–116 is elusive and difficult, but of a profundity that demands the closest study. His exposition is at once advanced and hindered by his aversion from reference to more systematic doctrinal discussions, for instance (to take a classical 20th century example), the issues raised in the argument between Hastings Rashdall and Peter Taylor Forsyth. Here again Hoskyns' strength is in the subtlety of his perception where New Testament distinctions are concerned—his responsiveness to what is being said, so subtly different and decisively more searching than its most obvious sense. His exegesis is animated by awareness of the preciousness of the familiar, of its parabolic indication of the creative omnipresence of God; yet these treasures (rich in themselves), are precarious, providing no resting-place, liable continually in human use and delight in them to the destructive infection of sin. Religion, law, government, sexual self-giving, the love of parent for child and child for parent, spontaneous service of one's fellows, responsible fulfilment of one's professional obligations, resolute struggle for justice for oneself and for one's fellows, protest against intolerable evils, disciplined forbearance in the face of oppression or legal injustice—one could continue the catalogue indefinitely; and always one finds ultimate ambivalence or the infection of sin.

Yet we have no other world than this in which obligations conflict with tragic consequences, where for instance the totally disinterested devotion of the artist (an analogue of the saint's love of God), may be the cause to others of pain and grief, of cruel neglect and indifference in respect of what they had every right to expect from him. The saint's own devotion may itself be achieved only in consequence of a sharp indifference to the claims upon him or her of those to whom he or she owes their very opportunity to begin the ascent of Carmel, to approach the outskirts of the vision of God.

It was Hoskyns' power as a theologian to glimpse the significance of Crucifixion—Resurrection for such predicaments. Thus he was enabled to find in Christ's passion less the ground of pessimistic renunciation of human hope than the promise that through the brutal bitterness of death tasted by the Son of Man for every man, confirmed in the glory of his Father by his resurrection from the dead, we may be assured that nothing is ultimately lost. 'If a grain of wheat fall into the ground and die . . .' Wakefield (as I have said above), is right to bracket with the early appreciative comments on the young Socialist's hope in 1916, the remarkable sermon on 'Quench not the Spirit of God', which he quotes extensively on pp. 63–64. As I have said, this sermon reveals a Hoskyns whose deep perception of the sense of the parabolic enabled him to find in an idealism that his right-wing political commitment too often encouraged him to dismiss with an almost cynical contempt, a veritable sign, albeit suffused with ambiguity, of the Kingdom of God. Certainly the road to that Kingdom was a *via crucis*; but the living signs of its promise were not lightly to be dismissed. In such dismissal there lay a pride as great and as damaging as the superior humanitarian optimism Hoskyns so often denigrated.

If Hoskyns' work on the Barth translation was fruitful for his theological development, helping to make him the creative theologian he undoubtedly was, it is arguable that the inspiration he found in Kittel and the Wörterbuch was less beneficial. It encouraged him to indulge in the sort of paradox Professor Christopher Evans quoted: 'It's all in 2 Peter and Jude'; it led him too easily to embrace the false *mystique* concerning the force of individual words in the New Testament, so effectively chastised by Professor James Barr. More seriously it led him to esteem too favourably the Nazi revolution in its early periods. His pupil, Richard Gutteridge, in an article in *Theology* for November 1933 (of which the author is now justifiably ashamed, but which is a valuable historical record of the euphoria which swept Germany in the early months of 1933), which Hoskyns himself vetted, saw promise for the future in a movement that celebrated its achievement of power, not only by the beginnings of a monstrous onslaught on the Jewish people, but by the 'burning of the books'. One is at a loss to know how the devoted husband of a Cambridge mathematician (for Lady Hoskyns was just such), could have failed to see the signs of sheer evil in the contempt shown for the work of, e.g. Dr Albert Einstein, and in the destruction of his epoch-making writings in the name of a supposed 'renewal of social health'. It is not clear how far Hoskyns repudiated the prostitution of academic learning, displayed in Kittel's monstrous pamphlet *Die Judenfrage* (1st edition 1933; 2nd edition 1934). It may be that he allowed his personal friendship for the father-founder of the Word-Book, and his narrowly aristocratic impatience with left-wing idealism, to blind him to the ghastly implications of Kittel's admittedly urbane essay in preparation for the Nuremberg Decrees of 1935. We can only deeply deplore the Toryism that blinded a great theologian, for Hoskyns was undoubtedly such, to the growing menace of a revolution that he came perilously near construing as a route to the renewal of a country he knew well.

If Kittel and his associates encouraged Hoskyns in an exaggerated sense of the unity of the New Testament writings, already set in this direction indeed by his own revolt against the seemingly pluralistic attitudes of Streeter and the Oxford school of source-criticism, it was Barth who alerted him to the depth of epistemological problems lying at the foundation of the New Testament documents; his sensitivity to these issues, raised by the Pauline epistles, as well as by the 4th Gospel, established beyond doubt his claim to greatness. Most importantly, he saw that these problems were theological, I had almost said ontological in their source; and here the theme Crucifixion—Resurrection was of pivotal significance. It was the movement of the life of Jesus from Galilee to Jerusalem to Galilee (to endorse the Markan tradition of the resurrection narratives, and to pay due attention to John 21) that was a movement from 'life to death to resurrection' which constitutes the ground of epistemological problems lying at the basis of Christian faith. And on this topic Hoskyns writes with a profundity reaching beyond most of his contemporaries. Thus, in a passage rightly quoted by Wakefield on page 70, he writes:

'The visible, historical Jesus is the place in history where it is demanded that men should believe, and where they can so easily disbelieve, but where, if they disbelieve, the concrete history is found to be altogether meaningless, and where, if they believe, the fragmentary story of his life is woven into one whole, manifesting the glory of God and the glory of men who have been created by him.'

This passage and the later one which Wakefield quotes on page 70 shows the profundity with which Hoskyns could write of faith, and the former reveals clearly the extent to which, for all his insistence on the way in which perception was transfigured by the resurrection-faith, he never lapsed into any sort of denigration of the concrete actuality of the historical Jesus. It may well be that this theme needs to be taken up again in the suggestive but tantalising section on the resurrection-narratives, and Davey's own very interesting essay on the problem of knowledge (pp. 222–234) would have benefited by cross reference to the seminal pages quoted by Wakefield from Hoskyns.

But there is much else to praise in this superb piece of editorial work. The chapters on government and the obedience of Jesus, and that of eating and drinking and the oblation of Jesus (pp. 257–275) require discussion in detail. The former needs to be complemented by a critical examination of the much misunderstood logion: render under Caesar—and the latter is very suggestive for Eucharistic theology.

The concept of obedience, with which Hoskyns makes great play, needs certainly to be sharply criticized in the light of work done by von Balthasar and others on the more inclusive theme of *kenosis*. Davey in his University sermon of 8th March 1942, so unfairly criticized by Professor C. E. Raven, who seems to have been blind to the width of Davey's concern (as wide as life itself), goes a long way in this direction, and it is tragic that he was never able to complete the work to which he was then setting his hand. If he was inferior to the late Dr J. F. Bethune-Baker as scholar, it is hard to resist the impression that he was manifestly the latter's superior as a creative theologian.

Wakefield's achievement as a biographer *is* beyond praise. He shows Hoskyns 'warts and all', and supplements his record with an illuminating vignette of his younger collaborator. It is good that he has included (pp. 66–70) reference to Hoskyns' appreciation of Cranmer's liturgical achievement. His theological understanding of Cranmer's intention shows deep perception far beyond that reached by contemporary eloquent champions of what they call the '1662 Prayer-book', concerned as they are far more with matters of personal aesthetic preference than with doctrinal issues. Hoskyns' Cranmer is a man whose serious convictions require equally serious discussion, and his comments on Cranmer's intentions, especially in 1552 (illuminated by his own familiarity with the homilies and deep study of the 39 Articles), demand most serious consideration, even by those who, like the present reviewer, are committed to a markedly different tradition of Eucharistic faith and practice.

It is touching and fitting to be continually reminded of Hoskyns' debt to his wife, Mary Budden. She belonged to a very different tradition from that in which Hoskyns, baronet and aristocrat, was confirmed by his years in Corpus between the two German wars; but she saw the depth and significance of the problems with which he wrestled, and gave him magnificent support to his tragic and premature death in his 53rd year, in June 1937.

Wakefield concludes his labours by a short and interesting personal epilogue (pp. 351–367). It complements the touching foreword by Dr Michael Ramsey; but neither quite do justice to the haunting seminal quality of the book, pointing beyond itself to perceptions that for all the work's christo-centric bias, are in the end radical and profoundly theo-centric. For beyond the whole area of its engagement lies (as Davey points out in his University Sermon), the ultimate mystery of the Trinity.

Note A

The depth of Kittel's guilt has been established in Professor Robert Ericksen's book: *Theologians under Hitler* (Yale U.P., 1985) in which he emerges as a more profoundly committed Nazi than the nationalist Lutheran *Dogmatiker*, Paul Althaus, and more coldly dedicated than the near lunatic figure of the philosopher Emmanuel Hirsch. It is tragic that Hoskyns fell under the spell of such a man, bemused it would seem by more than his admitted scholarship, and that he failed seemingly to allow Barth, the theological architect of the Barmen Declaration of 1934, to emancipate him.

Chapter 14

EDWARD SCHILLEBEECKX' CHRISTOLOGY

Jesus: an Experiment in Christology, EDWARD
SCHILLEBEECKX, e.t. Hubert Hoskin. Collins, 1979 pp. 767,
£9.00

Christ: *The Christian Experience in the Modern World*,
EDWARD SCHILLEBEECKX, e.t. John Bowden, S.C.M.
Press, 1980, pp. 925, £19.50

It is a commonplace to say that important principles of method
in philosophy and theology are often established, not in
laborious treatises on the methodology of these subjects, but by
the work of men and women who get their teeth into quite
fundamental problems. In my judgement this intellectual
phenomenon is well illustrated by the first volume of Father
Edward Schillebeeckx' massive work on the person of Christ. In
the concluding section of this very long but always interesting
treatise, the author puts his finger on a crux that is one of
method, but which is most effectively shown by a great deal of
his preceding argument to be very much more. One could
review his book by giving summaries of its various sections, and
pointing out matters of details, and of more than detail, on
which one feels oneself called to quarrel with the author. But it
is part of this book's achievement that it crystallizes certain
central issues in the area with which it deals, and does so in a way
sufficiently exciting to merit the author's claim to have
discovered, through the painstaking road on which his
erudition has driven him, something genuinely new.

What his procedure brings out is the depth of the problems
raised for any fundamental Christian theological thought, by

the dependence of such thought on a proper hermeneutics. Father Schillebeeckx is a member of the Dominican Order, and is too deeply schooled in the traditions of Aristotle and St Thomas to despise ontology in the strict sense. He will never dismiss Aristotle's preoccupations in the *Categories*, and the earlier books of the *Metaphysics*, as a waste of time. He is aware that there are certain concepts, for instance thing and quality, existence, truth, which we employ in discourse concerning any subject matter whatsoever. The sheer pervasiveness of these notions renders them peculiarly significant for theology. Yet how is this significance experienced? It is encountered in a relative historical context, and we have to define it to ourselves in respect of documents that belong to that context, which indeed have themselves crucially helped to shape it. They both bear witness to its beginnings, and themselves help not only to ensure its continuance, but more intimately and more profoundly to create what it is. Hence for one who is a systematic theologian, the importance of the closest possible engagement with the New Testament documents. Here, of course, continually Father Schillebeeckx gives hostages to fortune, and knows that he has to defend his own judgement in matters of acute controversy. I propose therefore to illustrate his procedure and to discuss it with reference to three examples that are obviously of great importance.

1 On pp. 311–12 Schillebeeckx makes to sum up his protracted discussion of Jesus' approach to his death in the following paragraph:

> 'This is a very important conclusion; for it means that even prior to Easter Jesus is saying, in effect at any rate, that the "Jesus affair" is to go ahead. This is not just a vision born of faith and based solely on the disciples' Easter experience; it is his self-understanding that creates the possibility and lays the

foundation of the subsequent interpretation by the Christians. There is no gap between Jesus' self-understanding and the Christ proclaimed by the Church. If we ask whether the disciples can be thought to have grasped what Jesus was getting at prior to the whole event of Easter, the answer must be on the negative side. But after the first shock of his dying, the memory of Jesus' life and especially of the Last Supper must have played a vital role in the process of their conversion to faith in Jesus as the Christ, the one imbued to the full with God's Spirit. That Jesus was right in understanding himself thus and was on to the truth when he saw his death as being somehow tied in with his mission to offer salvation cannot of course be legitimated as a fact of history; it can only be dismissed or accepted in faith. But that he did so is a fact of history hard to deny.'

I do not call this discussion protracted in any pejorative sense, but rather to insist on its thoroughness, its care and its restraint. It is not only that the author supports his conclusions by a remarkably impressive command of the most important recent treatments of the subject; it is also that he shows himself capable of striking a middle way between more facile extremisms. One may wish that he had given more attention to the political setting of Jesus' ministry; one may find a certain tendency to oversimplify in his treatment of some of the rival religious groups and attitudes prevalent in first century Galilee and Judaea. But where the central issue of the relation of Jesus' self-understanding to the crisis of his life is concerned, he insists that justice must be done to the following considerations.

He recognises that the story as it is told in the Gospels, is told from four very different points of view, even if the writers are all indebted to earlier, more generally homogeneous sources, whether written or oral, or both. He is clearly influenced by the work of the 'redaction-critics', and the way in which he traces the differences between Mark's and Luke's treatment of the disciples' behaviour during Jesus' last hours, has a freshness and authenticity that gives his study of this familiar material a value by itself. But Schillebeeckx nowhere neglects the rôle that must be assigned to the writers' organising conceptions, or to the play of creative religious imagination and intelligence at work in their presentation of received tradition to new readers. Yet he insists that behind this variety there lies the recognition that the catastrophe in which Jesus' ministry ended, however shattering to his entourage, was not unforeseen by the victim, and accepted by him as not only congruous with what he had taught, said and done, but as in some sense constitutive of what had gone before.

As the passage quoted above suggests, Schillebeeckx wishes to assign to Jesus' own self-understanding a rôle in the interpretation of his life and death which a very powerful strand in contemporary New Testament exegesis would rather assign to his disciples' elusive and mysterious Easter experiences, conferring by implication on the subjects of those experiences the supremely creative rôle in the interpretation of Jesus.

Yet as one reads the very careful pages by which Schillebeeckx prepares the way for this most important conclusion, one is made aware that he is possibly more than he himself acknowledges in debt to the ontological tradition in Christological reflection, encountered in one shape in the formative years of conciliar orthodoxy up to 451, and in another in the treatises, for instance, of Aquinas and Scotus, which he deliberately refrains from doing more than mention in passing. Certainly he justifies his claim to proceed in argument 'from below upwards'; yet he recognises that the choice of the foundations on which he builds, and from which he mounts his structure, is of crucial importance. He cannot be accused of the hermeneutical naivety with which the late Professor C. H. Dodd has been charged in respect of his late work *The Founder of Christianity* (Fontana); he continually insists on an element of profound agnosticism, not only where the student is concerned, but more importantly where Jesus' own self-understanding is at issue. There is a sense in which it belonged to the very substance of that self-understanding that its subject must await the disclosure of its ultimate secret by the Father. There is a sense in which the word 'open-ness' is the one that one finds oneself most often using in respect of Schillebeeckx' view of Jesus' attitude here. Moreover, the word is not being used in a sheerly metaphorical way, but rather to suggest the manner in which the ultimately transcendent is all the time allowed to insinuate itself into events of every sort, yet never allowing itself to usurp a control that obliterates concrete human detail. But that detail itself is mis-described if it is presented in ways that deliberately disallow this irreducible mysterious presence.

One particularly impressive feature of Schillebeeckx' work here is the length of time he devotes to detailed study of Jesus' teaching. The theme of the Kingdom of God is thoroughly explored, and by this exploration the author goes some way to prepare the way for a crucial aspect of his treatment of Jesus' self-understanding. Here again one may regret a certain lack of attention to the political setting of Jesus' ministry, and one finds oneself wondering what Schillebeeckx would have made of Sobrino's recent important work *Christology at the Crossroads* (SCM, 1978). But this is a relatively minor complaint, appended to one's expression of thanks for what the author has certainly achieved.

2   The discussion of Jesus' resurrection is again marked by Schillebeeckx' sense of the great importance of hermeneutical considerations, offset by his complex and subtle sensitivity to dimensions of those problems with which such procedures are powerless to deal. It is again a discussion that is difficult to summarise without serious misrepresentation. Thus for a large part of the time Schillebeeckx seems to regard the tradition of the empty tomb as having its origin in the devotional practice of pilgrimage to the alleged site of Jesus' burial in Jerusalem. Yet

his awareness of the deep difficulty and internal contradictions of the narratives seem to tell against too simpliste an interpretation of this critical option.

On p. 525 of his book Schillebeeckx writes as follows:

'But more important than this grammatical dissection is the proven point that all the early texts say it is God who raised Jesus from the dead. The emphasis is on God's saving action in Jesus of Nazarth.

'There are of course passages in which we read that "Jesus himself rises from the dead". Very often the meaning is still: Jesus has risen (from the dead) through the power of him who raised him up.'

The passage summarises the strongly theocentric emphasis of his whole treatment. The importance of 'open-ness' in his analysis of Jesus' self-understanding prepares the way for this decisive judgement, and indeed one might say that the clarity and firmness with which that feature of Jesus' self-awareness is grasped, owes a good deal to Schillebeeckx' discrimination of this crucial element in New Testament teaching concerning Jesus' resurrection. There is certainly, in my view, mutual support here, and yet there is no lapse into philistine assertion either concerning what the historian may confidently say happened, or did not happen, or into vague statements concerning alleged transformation of outlook on the part of Jesus' disciples unrelated to scrutiny of tantalisingly elusive details in available narratives, and seemingly unsupported by the unique occurrence or occurrences those narratives are concerned to present.

3   On pp. 578–579 Schillebeeckx writes:

'The reason for this is the dialectical tension between the conjunctural and structural aspects of the thinking; it is this tension in particular that makes each history ambivalent—a constant imperative to engage in interpretation, which itself stands within the ambiguity of history. This history with its ambiguity is surmounted, but not annulled, by our "time-consciousness", by means of which we do in some measure transcend the "lived" temporality, not, it is true, in a *conscience survolante* but still in an "openness", to the Mystery which encompasses all "history" '

This passage is quoted, in spite of its obscurity, to illustrate the density of Schillebeeckx' reflection in the concluding section of his first volume on the problems raised for him by his seriousness over the issue of historical relativity. He seems to me to end by identifying the question of the universality of Jesus' significance as the form in which for men and women today, the issue of his divinity is most effectively posed and faced. Is this man, belonging as he does to a particular culture at a particular date in human history, properly regarded as universally significant? Universal significance is, of course, a dispositional, and not an occurrent characteristic; (this distinction is very important and needs to be made clearly, if the argument is to be understood). The Easter experience of the first disciples is a *necessary* condition, but emphatically not by itself a *sufficient necessary* condition, for the raising of this issue in its earlier, less sophisticated forms. For it to have been raised at all, weight must also be given to the tradition of Jesus' self-understanding, the reflective experience of the Church as the years pass etc.

For us, however, the issue needs translation into different terms, and the category of universal significance, understood as a dispositional characteristic, is offered as the means to an effective formulation. This category possesses something of the ambiguity of a Kantian category; that is, it is neither fully ontological (in the sense in which Aristotle's categories certainly are), nor is it merely epistemic. For significance, if applicable to Jesus in Schillebeeckx' sense, must belong to him, and not simply enjoy the status of a quality that we impose upon him in thought and meditation, by use of free, unfettered, imaginative activity, dignified perhaps by the epithet inspired. It must, in fact, be the Father's gift to Jesus, partly schematized for earlier ages both by the crudely anthropomorphic tradition of his exaltation, and in the memories of those aspects of his human life which suggested him (in Professor C. F. Evans' valuable phrase), to be uniquely *capax resurrectionis*. But what such significance is in *itself* must always remain hidden, and unknown. The ways in which successive generations of believing men and women define its content for themselves are relative, even if we can distinguish an objectively valid relativity from the product of a merely capricious fantasising. Here again I am converting important distinctions drawn by Kant to the novel task of bringing out what I think Schillebeeckx is after.

His argument is intricate and subtle, undoubtedly awaiting completion in his second volume. In particular, one may hope to see him engage there with the very different approach to the central issues of Christology, presented in the third volume of Hans Urs von Balthasar's *Theodramatik* (Einsiedeln, 1978),[1] and in some of its author's earlier explorations of the theme of kenosis. What becomes of the concept of universal significance, if one finds in the concept of divine self-limitation the surest way towards the *arcana* of the Incarnation, and dares to posit receptivity as a Trinitarian attribute, providing, as it were, the ground in God as he is in himself, of this irreducibly unique and creative act of self-limitation? It does not seem to me that such a seemingly different approach necessarily involves the depreciation of Schillebeeckx' notion of universal significance; rather by complementing part of its emphasis, it liberates

---

[1] See my essay in the volume—The Analogy of Beauty (T. & T. Clark Ltd. 1986).

Schillebeeckx' Christology from any suggestion of its being a new style of adoptionism.

What is clear is that although Schillebeeckx eschews designed ontological excursus, he is (as I have repeatedly insisted), deeply aware of the commitment of the theologian willy-nilly to metaphysical judgements. He is, indeed, himself the practitioner of a very subtle style of metaphysics, revealed in the way in which he complements his hermeneutical preoccupation with bold expeditions into still more elusive territories. To read his first volume is not always to be satisfied; but it is to be filled with impatient eagerness to follow this courageous and yet always reverent spirit to the term of his most strenuous investigations. His work is of first-order quality, and he deserves his readers' gratitude and the authentic tribute of their respectful interrogative criticism in the places where he may fail, at least at first, to win their assent. No book less deserves condemnation by intellectually philistine ecclesiastical authority, making its verdict easy for itself by bland indifference to the crucial issues with which the victim of its uninformed judgement has most strenuously and devotedly engaged.

(A word of praise must be given to the translator, the Rev Hubert Hoskin. I am not in a position to assess its faithfulness to the Dutch original; but as one who has read Schillebeeckx' book in the earlier German translation, I can only express admiration for the way in which Mr Hoskin has laboured to provide us with a readable English version of this very long, but undoubtedly important book).

The sheer length and scale of Father Schillebeeckx' second volume *Christ: The Christian Experience in the Modern World*, must daunt any reviewer. It is not only the fact that Dr John Bowden's quite excellent translation runs to 923 pages, but that the author packs into those pages so much that merits discussion, both in respect of his central contentions, and in respect of the many more particular issues of exegesis etc. to which he refers almost in passing, and yet hardly ever fails to interest or illuminate by his comments.

I propose therefore to divide my review into five parts, but first to explain my reaons for selecting these topics, and not others, for discussion.

Firstly Father Schillebeeckx has included the word *experience* in his title, and therefore it seems necessary to scrutinise his analysis of the concept of experience in the first 80 pages of his book, and to do so in light of the ways in which subsequent sections of the work enlarge one's grasp of the denotation of the term, thus at the same time deepening one's sense of its connotation.

Then I will turn to the fascinating treatment given to the epistle to the Hebrews and the Gospel of John in this book. Certainly there is much that merits discussion in Schillebeeckx' treatment of Paul, including some quite minute linguistic studies, illustrating the seriousness of his concern with questions of language in the strictest philological sense. But it is clear that if all theologians are either Pauline or Johannine in inspiration, Schillebeeckx is among the latter, and though it is with regret that one turns aside, for instance, from discussing his interesting pages on the relation of Paul and James, concern with his central thrust constrains attention to the treatment of John and Hebrews.

Then I wish to turn to the treatment of human suffering in the later parts of this book, bearing in mind the way in which *experience* is understood by its author, and seeking to show both its strength and its likely limitations and weakness. Fourthly, it is surely desirable to help students of this very remarkable treatise by mentioning a few of the briefer discussions of matters sometimes relatively peripheral to its central concerns, but repeatedly valuable and deserving comment.

Finally I wish very briefly to say something of the extent to which this book fulfils the promise of its predecessor *Jesus*; by developing its themes and answering the questions it left open.

The first fifty pages of Father Schillebeeckx' text are devoted to epistemological issues, and in particular to the analysis of the concept of experience. It would, however, be a mistake for the reader to treat this section as if the topics with which it deals were disposed of once and for all. It is among Schillebeeckx' strengths as a thinker that he allows his own understanding of the method which he is using to be enlarged, and even corrected, in its actual employment; in particular it is only quite late in the volume that the reader achieves a full grasp of his notion of dialectic.

Schillebeeckx' understanding of Christian experience sees it as compacted of a number of distinguishable factors in complex inter-play one with another. The reader of his earlier work *Jesus* will expect strong emphasis on the historical and cultural relativity of the various moments in the development of this experience which, by reason of their formulated expression, have acquired a normative significance. It is not that he considers the intellectual, moral, and spiritual struggles of past ages as something over and done with; we have their legacies as part of our own patrimony, and provided that we do not claim the wrong sort of oracular finality for what has been achieved, we can discern repeatedly advances in insight that are permanently significant. We find such gains in the so-called letter to the Hebrews and in the Gospel of John. Thus where the latter is concerned, on page 380 Schillebeeckx writes:

'Perhaps the whole mystery of the Gospel of John lies in John's identification of the synoptic kingdom of God with Jesus of Nazareth.'

Certainly there is danger of loss as well as gain, and the author is sharply aware of the fact. But an advance in insight has been gained which illuminates in many directions, and will undoubtedly continue to do so. Indeed, as we shall see, Schillebeeckx practises himself discrimination in his use of classical sources, which enables the reader to learn from his example, and even on occasion to correct him by reference to his practice elsewhere!

The emphasis on relativity compels close attention both to the religious and intellectual assumptions of successive Christian communities, to the challenges and threats that met them from without, and to the conflicts, often related to the external menaces, which rent or threatened to rend them from within. Over all there loomed the *novum* which they believed to have been encountered in Jesus of Nazareth, and at times Schillebeeckx comes near identifying the experience he is analysing with so many efforts under the Spirit's guidance, to renew in significant form that continuing, inexpungable memory. Thus in the later part of the book, when he turns to discuss the problem of human suffering, the careful reader can discern delicately suggested correspondences between the conflicts that almost inevitably spring from serious engagement with such issues, and the more concentrated, yet always disturbing arguments, to which on his view of its origin, the fourth Gospel was intended as a response.

It is indeed in the long section which he devotes to that work, following the equally dense pages on Hebrews, that we can best appreciate Schillebeeckx' power as a creative theologian. There is a sense in which he seems in the end to see both works as engaged on the deepest level with the proper understanding of Christ's pre-existence. To say this is not to ignore the very many other issues with which he sees them concerned, or indeed to neglect the significant literary critical judgements that he passes on them. Thus it is suggestive to be told that Hebrews is not a letter, but much more a homily, or even a lecture. Again, on page 363, he suggests that in the fourth Gospel, the fifth, the

THEMES IN THEOLOGY

seventeenth, and the twentieth chapters, are literary masterpieces, but that other sections bear evidence of carelessness in composition. Towards the end of the book (p. 815), Schillebeeckx says that he cannot imagine any form of human knowledge that has no basis in perception. This remark inevitably recalls the long treatment of John XX on pp. 416ff. which in my judgement constitutes an admirable essay on one of the greatest passages in all Christian literature treating of the relation of faith to perception. Admittedly here we have a passage that treats of issues closely related to the problems of the transcendent and its representation; but the closeness of Schillebeeckx' attention to his sources enables him say a great deal of wide-ranging significance, without indulging his habit of taking refuge in self-indulgent reference to the theme of 'Jesus as eschatological Lord'. The way in which Schillebeeckx has recourse to this particular phrase is neither worthy of his stature as a theologian, nor indeed required to get him out of difficulties that he is treating more effectively elsewhere.

Where Christ's pre-existence is concerned, he has much to say of the importance in John, as well as in Hebrews, of distinguishing his status from that of alleged angelic beings. He lays great stress on the contrast of the earthly and the heavenly in Hebrews, and on the language of spatial movement in John. He writes as if both authors were urgently trying to de-mythologize their language, or to convert it into an indispensable instrument for representing the ultimate, free from the sorts of idolatry that its undisciplined employment could encourage. It is, of course, one of Schillebeeckx' greatest strengths as an exegete that he knows all the time that the works he is dealing with are many-sided, embodying arguments, implicit as well as explicit, on a whole number of issues. Thus, where the fourth Gospel is concerned, Schillebeeckx is convinced of the Palestinian-Jewish context of its origin, claiming indeed in several places that its Hellenism is akin to that of the group around Stephen. In pursuit of this judgement, he stresses the importance in the work's besetting concern with the vision of God, of the criticisms it embodies of claims made in the circles in which it was written, for Moses. It is impossible not to admire the ways in which Schillebeeckx strains to do justice to the many-sided character of the experience he finds encapsulated in the works he is studying; the cost it exacts from him in correspondingly critical response is very considerable indeed.

It is a weakness of his introductory section that he says almost nothing on such crucial questions in the philosophy of logic as the relations of word and concept, sentence and proposition. Much later in the work he draws most effectively on Thomas' commentaries on the Sentences of Peter Lombard in treating of the status of evil, (pp. 728, 891), and is clearly not therefore in blind revolt against the styles of the Roman schools; as always he is discriminating. In one place he remarks on the significance of the Platonic contrast between the one and the many for the judgement of the writer to the Hebrews on the relation between the priestly work of the one true priest who is Christ, and the multiple repeated cultic actions of the Levitical priesthood. He is certainly sensitive to the world of metaphysics. But the extent to which, in the fourth Gospel, metaphysical criticism of the mythological schemes of angels, heroes, etc. is itself being submitted to critical transformation in the light of the Christian *novum*, seems to elude him. It is significant here that he completely neglects the importance for John of the narrative-device of irony, with unfortunate consequences when, in the section on the life of grace and political power in the New Testament, he returns on page 581, in the third paragraph, to the Johannine Passion-narrative. Thus, even if one supplies this omission oneself, it is impossible to acquit Schillebeeckx of serious lack of insight at this point, although his balanced appreciation of Dr M. Lowe's argument in his article 'Who were the *Ioudaioi*?' (NTS 18, 1976, 101–130), on pp. 335ff. and 872f., should have helped him to penetrate deeply the political bearings of the passage in question. Again (and this is closely connected with the foregoing), he does not respond to the way in which John's bold, if sometimes hardly consistent uses of the term '*Son of Man*' reach their climax in the scene of *Ecce Homo*. Arguably the literal force of the Greek is: 'Look, the poor fellow. You cannot take him seriously.' But behind the contempt we must discern the procurator's presentation of the judge of all the world. 'Ye shall see the Son of Man' etc. Again irony and *double-entendre* do duty for the cruder advertisement of the presence of the ultimate provided by the miraculous embroidery of the Synoptic Passion-narratives. To write in these terms is to suggest that the dialectical movements of thought and experience that Father Schillebeeckx so excellently traces must include serious engagement with metaphysical tradition. In fact, in his long discussion of the understanding of Christ's priesthood by the writer to the Hebrews, he does succeed in bringing out the kind of intellectual tension that is set up when attention to narrative detail (and he cannot be accused of overplaying the circumstantial references to Christ's human life in that letter), is inserted almost intrusively into a carefully constructed scheme of the relations of temporal to eternal. Schillebeeckx excellently delineates the ways in which the near-contradictions in the concept of Christ's priesthood (and it is only in Hebrews that priesthood is predicated of Christ) are expressive of the need to hold together the mystery of his eternal pre-existence and the dependence for its constitution, of his present priestly role on the particularities of a human existence lived once for all, datably and locatably.

On p. 323 Schillebeeckx writes (with reference to the fourth Gospel):

'In speaking of the *Katabasis* or descent from heaven, that is, of the sending of Jesus by the Father, John is not presenting a theology of the Trinity, but a Christology.'

Yet further on in the same section, on p. 431, he writes:

> 'For all this it becomes clear that John puts forward a *functional* Christology, but not in the modern sense of this word. John's preference for verbs over nouns is very striking. For John, Jesus is really man, but in a unique, all-surpassing relationship with God. What John says and does reveals his person, that is, the mystery of his unity of life with the Father. In this sense, the function *is his person itself.*'

All the words italicised in this quotation are in italics in the original. In my judgement this paragraph is one of the most important in the whole book. It is a great pity that Father Schillebeeckx does not explain more clearly the sense in which he understands *function* and *person* as identical[2] He is saying something very important: but to make it plainer he needs to go on to treat of the ontology of relations in its bearing on Christology, and in particular on the way in which the Christian claim for Jesus transforms the understanding of the relation of the temporal to the eternal. Certainly, however, the argument which reaches its climax on p. 431 justifies the impatience he expresses towards the end of his work with the dogmatic assertion that in Christology the attractions of proceeding from below-upwards, or from above-downwards, are mutually exclusive.

In his long consideration of the problem of human suffering Father Schillebeeckx shows himself again a master of the field. There is, as often, much to praise in detail and judgement. He sees the value of Kant's *opuscula* as containing a criticism of Leibniz' theodicy more powerful than even the devastating

---

[2] Cf. von Balthasar's use of *Sendung* in Theodramatik III.

pages of Voltaire's *Candide*; he recognises the myopia almost inevitably springing from the quite intelligible concentration of the New Testament writers on the persecution of Christians. He strains to the limit to comprehend the ramifications of the contemporary scene, and to interpret the conflicts of present-day theologians and philosophers (not least that between some of the South American exponents of the theology of 'Liberation', and such European thinkers as Jürgen Moltmann), dialectically as divergent responses to its manifold demand and threat. His effort after comprehensiveness deserves praise; but inevitably it exacts its price of lapses into relative superficiality. Thus he fails to do justice to the complexity of Dr Karl Popper's philosophy of science, and indeed underestimates the many-sidedness of the logical empiricist tradition to which it belongs. It is not entirely insignificant that the name of John Stuart Mill does not occur in his remarkably wide-ranging index of authorities. Yet Mill, in the pilgrimage recorded in his *Autobiography*, provides the student with a classical reminder that the logical empiricist tradition is itself marked by the sorts of dialectical confrontation that Schillebeeckx finds in Christian history from the age of the apostles to the present.

Where human suffering is concerned, his positive insight is considerable. Here his agnosticism in soteriology combines with his brooding sense of the revelation in Jesus of Nazareth as a *novum* to enable him insist that the problem be stated not in general terms, but by constant, reiterated reminders of the concrete and particular. Certainly he is, as I have said, overwhelmingly aware of the ways in which the actualities of human pain determine different contemporary responses to the question (to use the language of Plato's Socrates) *peri hontina tropon chrē zēn*. Yet his admiration for Kant's critique of all theodicy stems from his awareness that no generalised intellectual debate gives answer to the innumerable Jobs of every age. And here, with characteristic insight, he turns to the

Gospel narrative of the sheer failure of Jesus, to which certainly his exaltation is an answer, but not such an answer as annuls the harsh actuality of the previous defeat. It is (I suspect) the author's intention to suggest here a humanly unbridgeable gap, but one whose recognition conveys the only ultimately consoling indication of a divine presence to our human extremities. The argument is not easy to follow, partly because while Schillebeeckx makes plain his preference for the Irenaean to the Augustinian tradition of the fall etc., (to this extent agreeing with Professor John Hick), he is equally insistent that the move across to the Irenaean tradition fails to rise to the finally unaccountable actuality, the intractable surd-element in human existence, that is there, inexpungably there, in the life of Jesus. Here he comes very near saying that an honest hermeneutic will take up into its profounder insights what is valid in older metaphysical styles. But what is such a hermeneutic? We have Schillebeeckx' practice to inform us. Its marks must surely include (as his does), a refusal to obliterate the unfathomable simplicities of Jesus by the alleged profundities of abstract argument.

There are very many points of detail to notice. Certainly in treating of suffering Schillebeeckx is right to refer to classical literature; but it is a pity that in seeking portrayal of human compassion in Greek literature, his strange neglect of Sophocles leads him to ignore the figure of Deianira in the *Women of Trachis*. The section (pp. 682ff.), in which he refers in quick succession to many ancient writers promises, but disappoints. The reference to Plato limps, and it is strange that there is no mention of the figure of Dido in *Aeneid IV*, when he makes appreciative quotations from Virgil. But I make critical mention of this passage because the very presence of these references is further evidence of the strenuous engagement of the writer with his theme, manifested also in, e.g. his remarks on *charis* in the Lukan writings, on the sense of *apodidonai* and *paredōken* (in John 19), on John 17 as the prayer of the shepherd, on angelological speculation. One could go on indefinitely.

In conclusion a word on the extent to which this volume fulfils the promise of its predecessor, and answers the questions with which it left the reader. The promise is certainly fulfilled by the wealth of material made available, and most certainly the treatment of human suffering to which I have done less than justice illuminates the concept of universal significance, so clearly crucial in *Jesus* as providing a bridge between absolute and relative. If the reader integrates what Schillebeeckx writes concerning Hebrews and John with what he says in this section, both the texture of his Christology and his understanding of authentic theological method become clearer. There is much more work to be done, however, and very tentatively I suggest the relation of time to Christ as a starting point,[3] a topic on which there is not a little profoundly suggestive material in this work.

But one's very last word must be one of profound gratitude to the author for a great contribution to the central themes of Christian theology. We are all of us in his debt. All readers in the U.K. must likewise express appreciation of the labours of Dr Bowden and the S.C.M. Press in making available this second volume for use and study here.

---

[3] We have moved a long way beyond Oscar Cullman's *Christus und die Zeit* (1947).

PART D

EPILOGUE

Lex orandi, lex credendi

In discussing the issue of divine impassibility, we do well to be guided by the Latin maxim, quoted above. That is to realize the two contrasted positions on this matter that have become familiar to generations of Christians, who have dimly, but surely affirmed in prayer and hymn what is in fact self-contradictory. We do not need to go further than the most familiar levels of common prayer and praise to recall this. Consider the following:

I

(1) *The hymns of H. F. Lyte*
      O thou who changest not, abide with me.

      Frail as summer flower we flourish;
      Blows the wind and it is gone:
      Yet while mortals rise and perish,
      God endures unchanging on.

(2) *The burial service of the Church of Scotland*
      Before whom the generations rise and fall

(3) O strength and stay upholding all creation,
       Who ever dost thyself unmoved abide.
                    (Ambrose: e.t.   F. J. A. Hort)

(4) 'may repose upon thine eternal changelessness'
                    (Evening prayer).

The language is, of course, saturated in metaphor. What

image is evoked by the suggestion that 'generations rise and fall'? It is often remarked that we spatialize temporal realities in order to think them; but here eternity is also invested with something akin to the Aristotelian *energeia akinēsias*. More simply: God is conceived as timeless, self-enclosed activity, totally immune from any sort of infection or disturbance *ab extra*. Nothing that can be represented by e.g. the metaphor of viral infection can touch Him; 'He abides unchanging on'.

Yet if by further metaphor, we think through this alleged immunity, we do not find it spiritually sterile; it is not to be dismissed as a thoughtless incapsulation of Aristotelian or Platonic metaphysics in a very different religious or theological context. Divine transcendence is a common emphasis in Judaism, in Islam, in Christianity. And it issues not only in a proper austerity of thought and imagination, but in a consoling sense that the changeless divine is unaffected in His substance by the changes and chances of this fleeting world, that He is as He is for our ancestors, for ourselves, for generations yet unborn, for the world, as it was, before life appeared, even (to stretch language) before time came into being with that world. His more special immunity from pain and suffering is seen as an aspect of a total self-containedness which is not to those who affirm it, an icy indifference, but rather a ground of security. Because the world is in external relation to Him, it cannot touch the substance of His being; its restless instability leaves His constancy unaffected.

II

Yet of course this is not the whole story.

(1)   There is no place where earth's sorrows
      Are more felt than up in Heaven:

There is no place where earth's failings
Have more kindly judgment given.
                    (F. W. Faber).

(2) 'who declarest thine almighty power most chiefly
     by showing mercy and pity'.
     (Collect from the Scottish Book of Common Prayer,
                    1929).

(3) 'whose nature and property is ever to have mercy and to
     forgive'.
          (Post-communion for Lent from the same book).

Faber's doggerel has often been criticized, and need not detain us, except as an extreme expression of our sense that we must exclude from God any likeness to a human despot, and suffuse our confession of His absolute authority with recollection of a tenderness at least as great.

But the other two quotations need far closer attention. Divine omnipotence is declared, by implication revealed supremely in 'mercy and pity'. Power is found where Paul found both wisdom and power, in Christ crucified, found there and therefore to be measured by reference to that disclosure. We must not allow our conceptions of transcendence, of divine self-containedness to be developed in such a way that by their very loftiness, they outrun continual correction by that standard.

In the post-communion we are arguably taken further along the same road: 'whose nature and property is always to have mercy and to forgive'. The term—property—is obviously a translation of the mediaeval *proprium*. This word stood for a category (in the Aristotelian scheme) that was to be located between those of secondary substance and accident. When we predicated manhood of Socrates, we were predicating in the category of substance: when we said of him that he was a philosopher, then we were predicating in that of property. For clearly his being a philosopher touched the stuff of what he was more intimately than his being of short stature etc. But of God it is said not only that it is his property to forgive, but that it is His nature. His readiness to forgive and to have mercy is grounded in, is indeed expressive of his very nature. From that readiness, manifested indeed dramatically in Christ, we affirm ourselves in touch with that which issues from his very substance. We rest in confession of a mercy that is not the thing of a moment, as affection may temporarily deflect a despot from his relentless egoism, but is as changeless as God Himself.

In fact study of the language of these two prayers reveals that even where there is clear reference to concrete, divine action, the ontological emphasis is sustained. We are encouraged at the risk of seeming contradiction, to invest the supposed divine self-giving with the constancy, the total immunity to change, that we found consoling in the metaphysical austerity of Ambrose's and Lyte's hymnody. It is indeed paradoxical thus to invest what is temporal with the character of eternity, what belongs to the world of chance and change with that of changelessness. More crudely to revert to Faber's doggerel, we find echoes of his sense that in Christ, the invulnerable made itself vulnerable, and this vulnerability is not something episodic, but belonging to heaven itself.

III

What we have done is little more than probe familiar religious language, where metaphysical ontology is used to achieve in part deliverance from metaphor, in part to secure what can only be metaphorically conveyed. Lyte's hymnody conveys the consolation to be found in austerity of imaginative conception; if the traditional metaphysical inheritance of the Platonic and Aristotelian schools has done nothing else for religious belief and practice, it has shown how such intuitive perception may be given the firm structure of definite, formally precise expression. Yet in Christian experience, such affirmation of the self-containedness of God is abstracted from other styles of compassion, in which ontological and dramatic are explicitly or implicitly allowed to interpenetrate one another. It is as if the dramatic is invested with the quality of the changeless: or as if purpose that involves necessarily not only the positing of time, but action within its series is eternized. We are not unfamiliar with language that speaks of 'God's eternal purpose', and in so speaking, invests steadfast fidelity with the character of eternity, a contradiction that none the less conveys the sense that such purpose is not alien to but congruous with, and expressive of, his being as it is in itself.

Consider again this metaphor of immunity. For us immunity from this or that infection is something we must acquire, for instance, by inoculation, and not infrequently as something requiring, as in the case of tetanus, renewal, if the guarantee it conveys is not to be lost. Or if we speak of ourselves as immune now from this or that sort of distraction, or temptation, we are implicitly recalling a time when this was not so, and we were liable to be deflected from this or that enterprise, or to yield to this or that temptation. Even if we speak of built-in immunity, we are implying that it is something that does not touch the substance of what we are: at best a property, in the sense mentioned above. But when we speak of divine immunity, we are speaking of something grounded in and expressive of the divine self-containedness. Social workers have to train themselves, often painfully, not to become 'involved' with their cases, but to cultivate a certain highly specialized detachment, that is altogether other than indifference, but a quite necessary condition of their professional competence as 'carers'. So Reinhold Niebuhr, seeking to deliver the notion of divine impassibility from the apparent abstractions of metaphysics, spoke as God as needing to retain within himself the means of overcoming the disasters of world history. Thus in order as it were to be touched to intervention, he must be seemingly remote in self-contained isolation. Yet if we are to speak of intervention (taking for granted the presence of temporal succession to the divine awareness), it cannot be seen as the almost random movement of the *deus ex machina*, but continuous with and expressive of what God is in Himself. On such a view His invulnerability must be seen as something posited in the very act of creation as the ground of his vulnerability. For of course both vulnerability and invulnerability touch His relation to us.

At the heart of Christian theology, as an intellectual activity, there lies the continual interpenetration of dramatic and ontological. And this may be judged as involved in the very act of the Incarnation. For here we are involved with what is totally concrete, its details historically disputable, and at the same time with that for which ultimacy is claimed. The paradoxes of the life and death of Jesus are familiar enough: they are matters of historical and exegetical evaluation. We have to reckon continually with what is historically particular and contingent, and where the subject of these final reflections is most immediately concerned with that of failure. The rhetoric of *Christus Victor* should not be allowed to obscure that reality from our close awareness. The Cross and its historical *sequelae* are nothing, if not the place where divine vulnerability reaches its climax. For God is there decisively revealed as putting himself at the mercy of the world. In his own temptation Jesus is seen as having most painfully to achieve this sort of self-giving in Himself. For if it is revealed as in no way alien from, but rather congruous with and expressive of, the being of God as He is in Himself, there is agony in the human acceptance: 'Father, if it be possible'.

It is of course at this point that we see again the interplay of doctrines of Trinity and Incarnation. In the complex development of Trinitarian theology, one constant thread is surely the need so to conceive God as He is in Himself that this acceptance of vulnerability is judged as congruous with, indeed expressive of His being as He is in Himself. It is indeed totally innovative: yet where it reaches its point of concretion in the ministry of Jesus it bodes forth the reality of God's self-definition as Triune. The temptation of Jesus in the desert conveys the very presence in Him of this three-foldness of the divine being. For he sets Himself over against the Father in the power of the Spirit in as much as in eternity He is self-giving response to an eternal affirmation. Because God is archetypally and immutably self-limitation, and therefore love, He is able to assume into Himself not only the different limitations involved in creation, but the more sombre vulnerability involved in taking to Himself the substance of human history in Jesus of Nazareth. Yet the kenōsis, whose depths we have not begun to plumb, is not strange or alien to His being, but the declaration of its substance and the disclosure of the inwardness and manner of His power.

We may seem to have moved a long way from the beginning of this short epilogue. Yet it is the simplicities of very familiar devotion which by their durability should invite us to explore the rich, even contradictory implications of their statements. The paradox of the vulnerability of the invulnerable, of the invulnerability of the vulnerable remains, and something of the historical failure of Christianity in practice and in theory, stems from deliberate retreat from facing its implications. But the two-fold affirmation of divine transcendence and divine involvement that we have extracted from prayer and hymn at least advertises the work that needs to be done, and to be done by men and women who must never forget that they live in the century that has known the reality of Auschwitz, surely among the most terrible *sequelae* of Calvary, as its mystery has been distorted and perverted in the Christian ages. Can we now begin to allow perceptions never wholly obscured, indeed often in measure renewed, to discipline our imaginations enough to allow God in Christ Jesus to be their measure rather than our own individual or collective self-regard? We have treasure indeed in earthen vessels.

INDEX

Aaron, 11–12, 17–18
Acton, Lord, 3, 25
Adam-Smith, Sir George, 200–1
Aeschylus, 83
Alexander, Samuel, 191
Alexandria, 83
Althaus, Paul, 207
Ambrose, St, 177, 229, 232
Andrewes, Lancelot, 50, 58, 62
Anscombe, G. E. M., 157n.
Anselm, St, 58
Antigone, 105, 108, 131, 134, 154
Aquinas, St Thomas, 12, 148, 156,
   157, 211
Aristides, 179
Aristotle, 42, 147, 157, 209, 214
Arius, 58
Asquith, H. H., 53
Athens, 71
Augustine, St, 16, 42, 99, 183
Auschwitz, 71, 235

Bach, Johann Sebastian, 169–70
Balliol College, Oxford, 59
Barmen Declaration, 207
Barnes, E. W. Bishop of
   Birmingham, 2
Barr, James, 204
Barth, Karl, 152–3, 158, 198–9,
   200n., 201, 204, 207
Baxter, Richard, 2, 84
Baynes, Norman H., 105
Béarn, 93
Beck, General Ludwig von, 115–16
Begin, Menachem, 58
Bell, George, Bishop of Chichester,
   106–7, 108, 124
Bennett, Jonathan, 38
Benson, Father R. M., 97–8

Benson, Robert Hugh, 194
Berkeley, George, 61
Bérulle, Cardinal Pierre de, 89, 92,
   98–100, 101, 103, 104, 108
Best, Geoffrey, 114–15
Bethune-Baker, J. F., 206
Blanshard, Brand, 61, 65, 68
Bloch, Ernst, 163
Blunt, Anthony, 168–9
Bodin, Jean, 96
Boer War, 59
Boethius, 15, 185
Bolyai, János, 45
Bomber Command, 124
Bonhoeffer, Dietrich, 148
Borromeo, San Carlo, 58
Bosanquet, Bernard, 53, 59, 60, 64,
   65
Bouteville, 102
Bowden, John, 216, 226
Boys-Smith, Rev J. S., 54–6, 62,
   66
Bradley, F. H., 56, 63, 66
Bremond, Henri, 88, 101
British Council of Churches, 111
British Idealists, 50–68
Broad, C. D., 64n.
Bruch, J. L., 27, 67
Brutus, 179
Buckingham, Charles Villiers,
   Duke of, 93
Budden, Mary (Lady Hoskyns),
   207
Bull, Hedley, 106
Bultmann, Rudolf, 77, 150–1, 163,
   175, 199
Bunyan, John, 148
Burckhardt, Jacob, 105
Burke, Edmund, 53, 125
Butler, Geoffrey, 198
Butler, Joseph, 62